A History of
Hallmarks

St. Dunstan
*Statue in gilded
wood of the
Patron Saint of
the Goldsmiths'
Company, late
17th century.
Formerly the
figure-head of
the Goldsmiths'
Company's
Barge.*

A History of Hallmarks

WYNYARD R.T. WILKINSON
F.S.A.Scot.

QUEEN ANNE PRESS
LONDON

Design by Alan Coombes

Hallmarks by Strata Design

Published by Queen Anne Press Ltd
12 Vandy Street, London EC2A 2EN

Filmset in Monophoto Apollo by Tradespools Ltd,
Frome, Somerset
Printed in Great Britain by Fletcher & Son,
Norwich

CONTENTS

to Michael Clarke

My grateful thanks to the following for
allowing use of their material and
providing information:
Mr. J. S. Forbes and Miss Hare of the
Worshipful Company of Goldsmiths

and to Giles Eyre for his support.

W.W.

INTRODUCTION

Anyone undertaking the study of a subject concerned with the applied arts for the first time will usually find it very much harder than first envisaged. There are two main reasons for this. Firstly, because they are 'applied' arts, much about the subject can only be learned from direct contact, and often only from handling. Secondly, to learn the general background to the subject the student has to study books written by experts who often take much for granted in their search for scholarship. Some books, therefore, may confuse the student.

The object of this small book is to provide a simple background to the history and development of the silversmith in Britain, and to show as simply as possible how hallmarks were evolved and how they should be read.

I hope that it achieves that object.

GOLDSMITHS

In order to reap the full rewards from an interest in silver it is helpful to know something of the background and origin of any piece that may be examined.

Silver was one of the first known metals. Its unique colour distinguishes it from other metals or alloys. Silver is harder than gold, which makes it more practical as a metal for everyday use, and it takes such a high polish, that the Romans used it for making mirrors.

The mining of silver in Europe can be traced back to about 3000 BC. The ore contains a small proportion of silver, or quartz with silver embedded, again probably in relatively small quantities. Before the introduction of explosive materials, the ores had to be obtained from the rock-face either by men with picks or more often by the ingenious method of heating the rock with fire and then dousing it with cold water. The sudden contraction made it crack so that the ore could be more easily removed.

It seems that at first, at least in Europe, silver was only a by-product of lead-mining. There was very little practical use for either metal. In the course of the next thousand years (3000–2000 BC) silver began to be recognised as a precious metal and, probably because of its lustre, came into use for coinage. At about this time silver acquired a magical significance. It became associated with the moon in much the same way as gold became associated with the sun.

Both silver and gold have been mined in Britain since Roman times, although even then they were never found in significant quantities. Mining of silver and gold continued in Britain on a commercial scale into the eighteenth century when silver mined both in Wales and Lancaster was used for coinage.

The extraction from the ore and purification of silver

is made very complex by the large number of different forms in which it is found. The silversmith of antiquity simply burned his lump of galena until he was left with lead oxide and a lump of silver; with practice he learned that as the lead melted at a lower temperature than the silver he could pour off the molten lead, leaving the silver behind. More efficient processes were developed during the last century. One is a method of production by electrolysis. The silver in the ore is converted chemically into a soluble solution and then electronically or chemically precipitated from it to render pure metal. Another is to amalgamate the silver in the ore with another metal (usually mercury but sometimes zinc). This separates it from the lead in which it is embedded. The new amalgam is then distilled to produce pure silver. For both these processes the ore has to be made into a powder first.

After the production of the ingot silver the most important factor is transforming it into something useful, whether it is to be used in coinage, for silversmithing, jewellery, or even photography.

The social status of a silversmith in the second half of the twentieth century is something of a curiosity – the specialised artisan. This has not always been the case. During the centuries when much of England was subject to Viking supremacy, the silversmith was regarded as a leading citizen of the highest order, responsible among other things for the production and control of coinage in his particular area. After the Norman conquest the silversmith found a new rôle in society. He often acted as banker and pawnbroker, as well as producing silver and jewellery for sale. This acquired business acumen made him a valuable asset to a form of government that was based on the power of men and lacked any form of economic understanding. His technical and administrative powers in addition to his artistic prowess meant that at a time when an already inefficient form of government was becoming increasingly complicated, he was one of the few citizens capable of keeping up with its changes and comprehending its intricacies. This achievement put the silversmith in a strong position in relation to the community. It gave him influence to which he had never before aspired. The result of this sudden power was that silversmiths were as likely to be found administering new building projects, arranging the finance and the payment of the workers, or supervising at the mint, as they were to be found in their own workshops producing plate for the houses of the nobility.

This social and monetary power gave rise to the formation of a guild of silversmiths in London by 1180. The system of guilds had been slowly developing in Britain and on the continent of Europe from about the seventh century, but it did not fully develop and expand until the Middle Ages. Under the guild system the workers at a particular craft were divided into masters, journeymen, and apprentices. There was no way an apprentice could become a master without first going through the stage of journeyman, i.e. being paid for a day's work, which an apprentice was not. The guilds offered the right to the independent exercise of a trade in return for membership. Guild membership carried with it the privileges of citizenship. The guild protected its own particular craft for members and guaranteed a local market. It also ensured that customers were protected by demanding that its members possessed the proper qualifications and that the work they produced was of reasonable quality. The guild was almost immediately fined by the King's Court for being established without a licence from the King. However, it appears that by this time the guild was already powerful enough to ignore the order. The fine was never paid.

The earliest English ordinance relating specifically to goldsmiths was brought about by the selling of sub-standard plate to the household of Henry III. This legislation, 'De auro fabricando in Civitate Londoniarum', dates from 1238. It not only set standards of fineness for gold and silver but commanded the Mayor and Aldermen of London to select six 'discreet' goldsmiths, known as wardens, to superintend the craft and be responsible for seeing that all work carried out in the public street was with silver of no worse fineness than that used at the mint. There are still wardens at Goldsmiths' Hall to this day.

During the thirteenth century there was great rivalry between the rapidly growing craft guilds in London. This led to frequent rioting between members of different guilds. The most notable occurred in 1267 when the members of the Goldsmiths' Company had a pitched battle with the members of the Tailors' Company. About 800 men were involved. Some were apprentices. Many were neither goldsmiths nor tailors, but paid rabble. The result of this affray is uncertain, but it is known that the bodies of the dead from both sides were thrown into the River Thames and that those unfortu-nates arrested by the bailiffs were hanged as an example to others.

During the following two and a half centuries the Goldsmiths' Guild continued to expand its wealth and influence. Indeed, before 1524 there were an amazing 17 goldsmith Lord Mayors of London. On 30 March 1327 the Goldsmiths' Guild was given its first Royal Charter, empowering it to enforce the law with the help of the

Sheriffs and Lord Mayor of London. One important effect of the charter was to place a considerable amount of restraint on goldsmiths working in the provinces. The charter, and indeed an Act of 1300 relating to goldsmiths, made it quite clear that provincial goldsmiths were expected to send all their work to London to be tried by the wardens before selling it. This proved to be destructive to provincial crafts. There was little advantage in a customer ordering a piece from a probably inferior local goldsmith if it had to go all the way to London and back, when he could order the piece directly from London. The goldsmiths' charter was renewed by both Richard II and Henry IV who extended the goldsmiths' sphere of influence to cover the gold and silver work of cutlers.

There is a revealing paragraph in a Statute of 1403, which has since been repealed. This not only mentions some of the more common frauds perpetrated by the goldsmiths but lists a quantity of the smaller items that were at that time being made in precious metals: 'Fraudulent artificers, imagining to deceive the common people do daily make locks, rings, beads, candlesticks, harness for girdles, hilts, chalices, sword pommels, powder boxes and covers for cups of copper and latten (tin-plate) and the same overgild and silver'. The same Act made it illegal for a silversmith to gild base metals with the exception of ornaments for the church, and even these only if some part was left bare. Fraud in the metal was not all that was worrying the authorities at this time. Silver-gilt was often sold for more than double the price of a piece of silver of equivalent weight. This led to a price ceiling on silver-gilt wares of £2 6s 8d (£2.33) for a troy pound (373 g). The penalty for abusing this law was either to pay a fine to the value of the piece or to forfeit the piece itself.

On 30 May 1462 Edward IV issued the fourth charter of the Goldsmiths' Craft of London. This confirmed the charter of 1392 and gave the craft the right as a body corporate to use a seal and hold land. It also broadened its powers of regulation over all 'sorts of gold and silver manufactures' in the city of London and its environs, including all fairs and markets and in all places where it was 'exposed for sale throughout the Kingdom of England'. The existing power of the guild was thus substantially confirmed.

The only other change in the jurisdiction of the Goldsmiths Craft came in a Statute of 1477, in which the Goldsmiths' Company was given powers to fine and imprison any goldsmith found to be guilty of fraud and to seize and destroy any unlawful work.

The Reformation of 1539 was the next historical incident to have an effect on the goldsmiths, and indeed on the guild. In 1540 the craft was forced to destroy the all-important effigy of St. Dunstan that had decorated the entrance to the Goldsmiths' Hall in London.

St. Dunstan, patron saint of the Goldsmiths' Company and son of a West Saxon noble, was born in 924. He was educated by Irish priests at Glastonbury Abbey before joining the court of King Athelstan. He was banished from the court for 'practising the unlawful arts' after which he lived for a while at Winchester with AElfheah who persuaded him to become a monk. He returned as a monk to Glastonbury where he built himself a cell five foot long by two and a half feet wide. There he prayed and had 'heavenly visions'. In keeping with the convention that a monk should combine his devotional routines with a craft, Dunstan became a goldsmith. He made plate for use outside the abbey as well as the chalices, censers, and crosiers that would have been required within it. Legend has it that while working one day at his forge he was visited by a man who wanted to order some plate. Dunstan immediately recognised the man as the devil in disguise and seized him by the nose with his red hot tongs.

Dunstan became involved in politics when he was appointed Abbot of Glastonbury in 945. This meant that for the next 14 years he was alternately in and out of favour, depending on who was king. At one point he was exiled to France where he was so impressed with the Benedictine order of monks that he was later responsible for its introduction in England. With the accession of Edgar in 959, Dunstan was appointed Archbishop of Canterbury. His main political ambition at this time was the welding of the Danes and the English into one nation. He was responsible for the removal of secular clerks from the monasteries and ruled that clerical celibacy should not be compulsory but that a married priest should lose the privileges of his order. He died in 988. St Dunstan's day is 19 May and the beginning of the goldsmiths' year; for this reason London date letters run from 22 May to 21 May the following year.

The accession of Henry VIII and the influence of his extravagant style of living was to have an important influence on the fortunes of the goldsmiths for the whole of the sixteenth century. Henry VIII was unfortunate in that the huge quantity of treasure built up by his father was falling in value after the introduction of quantities of silver and gold from Spanish South America. However, it was not until 1523, when he had to pay for the French war, that Henry ran out of money.

The consequences of this were drastic by sixteenth century standards. A graduated form of taxation was introduced. But even this proved insufficient. In 1526

15

the coinage was debased for the first time in English history, at great profit to the Royal coffers. So successful was the experiment in terms of increased revenue that in 1542 the silver content of the coinage was dropped to 83 per cent; in 1544 to 50 per cent; and in 1545 to a miserable 33 per cent. This enormous fall in the value of money meant that the price of sterling silver plate soared. The customer then had to provide the silversmith with the requisite coin for the piece to be manufactured and the silversmith charged for his workmanship in addition.

The dissolution of the monasteries in 1538 and their subsequent despoilation was another huge source of revenue for the Royal treasury. Thousands of ounces of silver were taken from all but the smallest establishments. This also affected the silversmiths. They were asked to re-model the chalices of the old order to conform to the simple communion vessels of the new. But this practice deprived them of much of their licence to exercise full creative imagination.

In 1551 the silver content of the coinage dropped to a mere 25 per cent. None but the extremely wealthy could afford plate at four times its cost in 1525. But with the virtual re-establishment of the sterling standard in 1552, the door was opened for a new fashion for monarchs to order – not only plate and jewellery for their own use but also as diplomatic presents to other Courts. Some idea of the quantity and magnificence of the plate given away during this period can be gained from seeing the collections in Moscow and Leningrad.

The anti-inflationary measures introduced by Elizabeth I, which included the withdrawal from circulation of the debased coinage, led to a gradual increase in prosperity and therefore to an increase in the demand for plate. Surprisingly, this new prosperity had some unpleasant effects on the ever wealthier Goldsmiths' Company. It was often pressed for large loans for the monarch. In 1618 it had to find the vast sum of £14,000, supposedly for arrears of rent for 60 years.

In 1622 there is an interesting Royal declaration in which the King expressed his disapproval of the fact that there were other traders working alongside the goldsmiths in Goldsmiths Row in Cheapside. He demanded that 'the houses and shops there should be furnished and supplied only with goldsmiths for the continuance of the beauty and ornament of the chief street of this our city and so to restore it to its former splendour'.

It is interesting to note that it was probably this lack of confidence in the security of monies deposited at the Tower of London that led to the development of the modern banking system. In 1640, after Charles I had threatened to confiscate all the bullion lodged at the Tower, the merchants deposited their money with the goldsmiths of Lombard Street who were already well equipped for keeping valuables under safe supervision. There, goldsmiths paid interest at five per cent on all money deposited with them and then lent it out at rates up to eight per cent, the legal limit.

With the civil turbulence that started in 1624 and the almost immediate return to the continent of the foreign goldsmiths working in London, the craft entered a lean period. The records show that very little plate was made during the following four years. This was probably not just the shortage of money during war but because the enforced loaning or confiscation of plate was one of the main sources of income for both sides during the English Civil War. It is interesting that the warrants used to levy the forced loans for Charles I in 1632, name a sum of money but state that silver plate was acceptable as an alternative method of payment (touched plate at five shillings and untouched plate at four shillings and four pence per ounce). This showed that at least the Parliament of the King recognised that silver plate might be hallmarked or unhallmarked, and that the extra worth of the guarantee implied by the hallmarks was as much as 15 per cent. It is especially interesting that the effective statute in 1643 was that of 1575 which did not then regard hallmarks as a necessity.

Thus the first half of the seventeenth century was bordering on disaster for the Goldsmiths' Company. It had to sell plate to pay forced loans from the exchequer and the guildhall was taken over and used by Parliament as its treasury for the duration of the civil war. The smiths had little work because both sides were melting plate to make coin to pay their troops. With the end of the war and the renewed availability of bullion most of the patrons of 20 years earlier had fled abroad or perished in the conflict.

Fortunately for the goldsmiths the puritanical enthusiasm of the early 1650s diminished as the country recovered from the effects of the war. Once again they became prosperous. By 1660 the craft had already recovered its position of 20 years earlier. With the return of Charles II in 1660 together with a new and luxurious way of living and a large foreign entourage there was again a period of great prosperity for the Goldsmiths' Company and its members. Not only was there an influx of extravagant design from the continent, but for the first time London was establishing itself as the major trading city of Europe. Trade was conducted with Africa, America, and Asia as far as China.

This trade had the secondary effect of producing a

Set of 'Standard' weights, belonging to the Worshipful Company of Goldsmiths. Made together with 56 other sets and an 'Exchequer Standard' set in 1588 to standardise the weights in use throughout the country. This set cost £3 8s 1d (£3.40½p) to make. They remained legal standards for 236 years until being replaced in 1824.

new class of rich merchant, who logically wished to imitate the members of court by having his house furnished with plate of all sorts. The way of life of the upper classes, and indeed every strata of society, was rapidly changing. The strict order of medieval England was fast vanishing in the face of new discoveries. Tea, coffee and cocoa were introduced into the country. Tobacco became more popular and table manners more refined when forks were used for eating. The new affluence spread downwards rapidly. It was common for taverns to have silver punch bowls, flagons, and tankards. Because so much valuable plate was exposed in public places more taverns were robbed. But an Act of 1695 forbad the public exposure of any plate except spoons.

Surprisingly, the worst thing that happened to the goldsmiths in the late seventeenth century was the result of an ill-judged action by the King, whose restoration had done so much good for the goldsmiths. In 1672 Charles II closed his exchequer. This had disastrous consequences for the leading goldsmiths because they had been in the habit of lending their customers' money to the exchequer and now found themselves with the funds effectively frozen and without interest.

The huge increase in the amount of manufactured plate meant that the mint often found itself suffering from a shortage of bullion. It was this, coupled with the large number of coins in circulation that had been clipped by greedy owners that led to the new coinage of 1697 and the legislation that accompanied it.

Parliament's answer to the vast quantity of coin being melted to make plate (in the years 1695–6 the Goldsmiths' Company assayed and marked over half a million ounces of plate) was to introduce new legislation. The statute was cynically entitled: 'An Act for encouraging the bringing in of wrought plate to be coined'. The effects of this statute were many and far reaching. It raised the standard of wrought silver from the sterling standard to a new standard called, 'the Britannia standard' – 958.3 parts pure silver in a thousand, rather than 925. With the new standard new marks were introduced to indicate its use. The Britannia standard remained obligatory until 1719, but after 1 June 1720 either the old sterling standard or the Britannia standard were permitted to be used.

During the remainder of the eighteenth century there was a drastic change in the social status of the goldsmith, as the industrial revolution changed the whole basis of English society. No more was he a leading member of society often to be seen at court, but now just another member of the new order of worker-craftsmen. This changing rôle did not, however, prevent the emergence of some brilliant goldsmiths, either as specialist smiths producing large quantities of a particular product as well as their normal wares, or as master-craftsmen whose work is, even to the uninitiated, of exceptional quality. These men and women may be regarded as the last of the real goldsmiths. They, like so many other craftsmen, were to be absorbed into the world of machine and workshop.

The improved mechanical techniques of the second half of the century led to a new class of cheaply produced silver at a period when a new class of people was emerging who could aspire to just that. Machines were developed that could roll silver so thin that when it was stamped out and made into something large like a candlestick the item had to be filled with resin and weighted at the base to give it stability. Most of the 'new' machine-made items, almost mass produced, were made in Sheffield or Birmingham. The goldsmiths of London continued much as before. Their more expensive hand-made wares were much finer than the wares of their rivals and thus continued to appeal to Court and the upper classes.

The extravagant patronage of the Prince Regent at the end of the eighteenth century came at the right time – when silversmiths were combining the best of the improvements in manufacturing methods with the exciting vogue for the taste of earlier civilisations, whether Indian, Roman, Chinese, Greek, Egyptian, Mooresque, or simply old English Gothic. All these were used at once in varying degrees for the full 40 years of the Regent's influence and reign. During this period the factory took over much from the individual maker. However, often pieces bear only the name of the nominal goldsmith, and probably senior partner.

After 1830 the factory came even more to the fore. Often factories would produce not one item, but a series of parts for articles made up elsewhere – handles, feet, spouts and so on. The styles of the next 70 years are often looked upon as being almost without merit, but they tended to follow two courses. One was a definite search for a feeling of antiquity, as brought out in the Gothic revival. The other was a search for contemporary archaeology which was later followed by a fascination for the Far East after the opening of Japan towards the end of the century. The Art Nouveau movement was the result of a reaction against factory work. Pieces were made by individuals who, as soon as their movement became successful, were forced to open workshops to keep up with demand. This revival came to an end with the outbreak of war in 1914.

HALLMARKS

Marks have been found on Roman and Byzantine silver indicating that some form of quality control system was then in use. But, it was not until the Ordinance of 1238 that any form of legal control was introduced in England. This was followed in 1300 by a further Ordinance which purported to influence 'all goldsmiths of England, and anywhere else in the Kings dominion' (this last meaning occupied France). It set the 'touch of Paris' as the fineness for gold, which is about $19\frac{1}{2}$ carats, while setting the standard for silver as 'sterling', or the same as money.

There are several explanations of the origin of the word 'sterling'. It has been said to be derived from silver coins minted in Saxon times which bear the image of a starling. Another explanation is that it is taken from coins bearing a star minted by the Normans in France; or that because the trial of the coinage was held every Easter that the word was derived from Easter. The most convincing explanation is that it is derived from the 'Easterlings', money makers brought to England by Henry II from Eastern Germany to improve the quality of the English coinage. Whatever the derivation, the term appears in the Ordinance of 1300 and has remained in use ever since. It means that the metal is 925 parts in a thousand pure.

The Ordinance of 1300, having fixed the standard, directed that no vessel of silver was 'to depart from the hands of the workers' until it had been assayed by the guardians of the craft (as appointed in 1238) and marked with the leopard's head. It continued: '. . . and the guardians of the craft go from shop to shop amongst the workers assaying that their gold be exactly like the aforesaid touch, and that they find any worse than the touch, that piece be forfeit to the King'. Provision was then made for one man from each of the 'good towns of

*Early print of interior of
a goldsmith's workshop.*

England' to be sent to London to collect his leopard's head punch '. . . and if any goldsmith shall do otherwise than as aforesaid it is ordained that he be punished by prison and by ransom at the kings will'. It was not until 1856 that this Ordinance was repealed. It had been law for over 550 years.

Ordinances and statutes relating to gold and silver are almost unique. Even after they are repealed they cannot be considered irrelevant. Wares produced while they were in force will have survived the Acts themselves and, must therefore be considered lawful so long as they conform to the regulations in force at the time of their manufacture.

The next important development for the marks is the Statute of 1423, which was entirely devoted to silver. It confirmed that the correct standard to be used was sterling and goes on to say that 'no workmanship of silver is to set to sale within the bounds of the City of London before it be marked with the leopard's head, if it may reasonably bear the same, and *also* with the sign or mark of the worker who made it'. Seven towns, apparently chosen because of their importance as centres of communication which made it easier for plate to be brought to them, were set up as assay towns. Each had 'divers touches according to the ordinance of the mayors, bailiffs, or governors of the same towns'. They are: Bristol, Coventry, Lincoln, Newcastle-upon-Tyne, Norwich, Salisbury, and York.

It was also laid down that no worker in silver within the Realm of England where no touch was ordained (not close to an assay town) was to work silver worse than sterling or put it up for sale before his own mark was on it. The statute laid down heavy penalties – double the value of the offending article – should the Keeper of the

Touch mark anything that was later found to be sub-standard. This happened in 1664. It was discovered that a cunning worker at the assay office had been taking the punches home with him to mark substandard plate belonging to friends with sterling hallmarks.

The Statute of 1423 was not repealed until 1953. For that period it remained the basis of all law on hall-marking. Subsequent Acts were intended as a dis-incentive to fraud, since the terms would be fresh in the minds of the workers.

In 1477 another Statute was enacted. This was the first of many which, while making little or no change to the general scheme, made minor alterations. In this case the gold standard was changed from $19\frac{1}{2}$ carats to 18. It also stated that the leopard's head sterling mark should be crowned, and that all goldsmiths who were 'aliens and strangers' to the London Company should be under its jurisdiction. It said that the Goldsmiths' Company should be 'charged and chargeable for the non-sufficiency of the Keeper of the Touch'. Apparently worried by this last provision, the company introduced a separate mark, a variable date letter, as a method of discovering the date at which a particular piece was marked, and thus who was the Keeper of the Touch at that time.

When Henry VIII debased the coinage to one third silver in 1544, the Goldsmiths' Company had to reassure their patrons that a similar worsening of standard had not befallen wrought plate. To do this they added yet another mark to those already in use, that of a lion passant 'guardant' (looking out of the punch, not looking forward). This mark was probably one of the most suc-cessful commercial guarantees ever devised as there are today many people who, with good reason, will not believe that a piece is silver unless it bears the lion passant mark.

Thus a piece of silver marked and made in London in 1545 would be marked with a maker's device, leopard's head crowned, date letter, and lion passant. These are exactly the same as those on a piece today, well over 400 years later, except that the leopard's head is now uncrowned and the date letter is in a different script.

Legislation introduced in 1575 is of double interest. Firstly, it was to remain unchanged until 25 March 1697, and secondly, while confirming the sterling standard and making the standard for gold 22 carats, it only said that a maker's mark should be put on to silver before it was sold or exchanged. There was no mention of hallmarks. This seems to indicate that it was not unusual to have unmarked silver, and that it was certainly not considered illegal to sell a piece bearing only a maker's mark.

The Statute of 25 March 1697 is quite unique. Not only did it change the standard and the marks to denote the standard but it specified the manner of the maker's mark. The new standard was 33.3 parts in a thousand more pure than sterling, or an extra eight pennyweights of silver in twelve troy ounces. This new standard was to be called 'Britannia'. The two compulsory marks that were introduced were a lion's head erased and the figure of Britannia, together with the regular date letter. It was declared that the maker's mark should be the first two letters of his surname.

The Plate Duty Act of 1719 was, as far as hallmarking is concerned, the next Act to have a direct effect on the London goldsmiths. One of the objects of the Act was to raise just over £300,000 for 'His Majesty's Supply', which was to be achieved through the sale of annuities. The annuities were charged on a plate duty of 6d ($2\frac{1}{2}$p) an ounce. This applied throughout the kingdom (Scotland had been incorporated since 1707). To pacify the understandably upset English goldsmiths, the old sterling standard was restored, while continuing the Britannia standard 'without obligation of restraint'.

However, the new Act still brought a squeal of anguish from the goldsmiths. Even with the restoration of the sterling standard, by the time they had paid the tax the cost still worked out at some 3d (1½p) an ounce more. Other complaints were that by the introduction of the tax the purchaser would be loth to bring in plate for refashion. Not only would he lose what was charged for the fashioning of his new piece, but also the cost of the duty, which was (according to a broadsheet published at the time) about the same as the goldsmith's charges for making the piece: '. . . and if 6d (2½p) per ounce be laid on Plate, the manufacturer must, for all weighty Plate, pay as much, or more, than he receives for the fashion'. It would appear that this figure was not entirely due to the optimism of the compilers of the broadsheet although it might be misleading to regard it as a reliable record. The diaries of the Earl of Bristol have interesting mentions of the cost of fashioning plate at the end of the seventeenth century in 1695: 'For two dishes made by Mr Chambers weighing 154½ ounces at 4d (1½p) per ounce for fashion and ten shillings (50p) for graving them and plate at five shillings and two pence (26p) per ounce £42 19s 9d (£42.98½)'; in January 1700: 'Paid George Lewis, silversmith, for two pair of plate andirons (a horizontal bar on short feet, with a pillar at the back placed on either side of a fire and used for supporting burning wood) being French plate at 5s 5d (27p) per ounce intrinsic value and 1d (½p) fashion in all 5s 6d (27½p) per ounce.' In 1703 he paid 10d (4p) an ounce for

COURTESY OF SOTHEBY & CO

*A set of three casters
made in London in 1723
and 1724 by Thomas
Bamford.*

29

the fashion of some dishes and plates.

The introduction of the 6d tax put the goldsmith who was commissioned to make a large piece of silver in a quandry: should he submit the piece for assay, pay the large sum of duty, and then submit the bill to a surprised customer, or find a way round the new legislation? There were two main ways of avoiding duty on pieces. The first was simply either not to mark the piece, or to strike it with only the maker's mark. This did not upset the customer. In most cases the metal used to produce the 'duty dodging' piece would have come from worn or out of fashion plate bearing hallmarks. The second method was more devious and confusing, especially to the modern dealer or collector. In some cases the goldsmith would carefully remove the mark from a piece before melting it, and then incorporate it in the manufacture of the new piece. This made a perfectly ordinary 1725 coffee pot look from its hallmarks as if it were made some 50 years earlier. Alternatively, on pieces with a relatively small base such as beer mugs, two-handled cups, coffee pots, and tea-kettles, the goldsmith would first submit a small and therefore light piece to the assay office, and then use it in the construction of the larger, hence the advantage of pieces with small bases where the 'transposed' marks would completely cover the base, – the marriage being concealed by the joint between the foot and the body. Another possibility in the case of completely unmarked plate is that it was manufactured by a smith who was regarded as an alien, and thus excluded from the privileges of British goldsmiths.

Another provision of the Act of 1719 was the return to the method of constructing marks from the first letters of the maker's christian name and surname. This meant that most makers had, for a while at least, two perfectly acceptable makers' marks which were in concurrent use.

The enormous amount of 'duty dodging' that was going on began to worry some of the leading goldsmiths despite the fact that they too participated in the practice. As a result they drew up a petition complaining that 'notwithstanding all previous Acts of Parliament and charters that great frauds are daily committed in the manufacturing of gold and silver wares for want of sufficient power to prevent the same'. The result was the 1738 Act 'for the better preventing of frauds and abuses in gold and silver wares'. For some reason this Act only applied to England, which is possibly a reflection on the less strict, but still effective way in which the different Scottish Burghs interpreted the law.

The 1738 Act had two main purposes. The first was to relieve the much overworked assay offices from the burden of having to try and mark thousands of small objects, thus also exempting them from duty. These objects are specifically mentioned, and include such items as buttons, toothpick cases, bells, rattles ('coral sockets'), and nutmeg graters. The second purpose of the Act was to eliminate the widespread practice of evading duty on larger pieces.

An extraordinary facet of the Act is that when dealing with the penalties for counterfeiting, it admitted openly that the penalty of £500 as introduced in 1700 was too great 'and hath been some occasion for persons escaping unpunished who have been guilty of counterfeiting' and reduced the penalty to a meagre £100. The penalty for fraud concerning marks was to be the subject of much experiment in subsequent Acts. Another provision of the 1738 Act, which specifically applied to the provincial assay offices, was that every goldsmith was required to have the punch he had had before 1719 destroyed, if he was still using it. The replacement was to be made in a different 'character or alphabet'.

For some reason the 1738 Act does not seem to have been as effective as desired. The 1757 Act revealed that duty was still not being collected, which the 1738 Act was designed to aid: 'the methods prescribed for ascertaining and collecting the said duty and for preventing frauds therin have been found ineffectual to secure payment thereof and the said Duty hath by reason of various frauds and evasions for some years greatly decreased'. In a fit of bureaucratic stupidity the 1757 Act replaced the 6d duty with a licence which every person 'trading in, selling or vending' silver or gold had to take out at the cost of £2. This had to be altered the following year because the payment of £2 was quite new to the smallworkers (makers of small objects), toymakers, and cutlers whose work had been exempted from duty in the 1738 Act. Accordingly, people selling pieces weighing less than 1/10 ounce of gold or $\frac{1}{4}$ ounce of silver did not have to take out the licence. Its cost to those who still had to buy one went up to £5 and was extended to refiners and pawnbrokers.

The Act of 1757 also changed, once again, the penalties for counterfeiting or abusing hallmarks. The lower penalty introduced in 1738 was abolished. It was made a felony punishable by death. One of the reasons for the constant changing of legislation concerning the counterfeiting and abusing of hallmarks was to keep the penalties fresh in the minds of the silversmiths, in the belief that if the penalties were to remain unchanged they would quickly be forgotten. The law was changed again in 1772 when the death penalty was replaced by a sentence of 14 years transportation.

In 1784, duty was introduced at a rate charged per

ounce on all goods. This included imported goods that were submitted for assay and marking. The duty, which started on 1 December 1784, involved the use of an additional mark in the form of a king's head. For the first year and a half this new mark was struck intaglio (incuse, as opposed to the other marks which are in cameo). This form of punch, however, like the rare drawback mark was not suitable for marking silver, because it was necessarily more detailed. The drawback mark was introduced at the same time as a form of export rebate, whereby a piece of silver on which duty had been paid and which was then sold for export, could be re-submitted, marked with a standing figure of Britannia, and the duty repaid to the goldsmith. It was not unusual for a piece of plate submitted for assay to be returned with expensive or unsightly damage which needed repairing before the piece could be set to sale. The drawback mark was withdrawn in July 1785, and the king's head punch was changed to 'in cameo' in May 1786.

The list of pieces exempted from hallmarking, and thus duty, was reviewed in an Act of 1790. The exemptions in the 1738 Act relating to silver were revoked, but not those for gold. A new list of duty exempt articles was substituted. The new list exempted all wares weighing under $\frac{1}{4}$ ounce, with the exception of 'necks, collars, and tops for castors, cruets, or glasses appertaining to any sort of stands or frames, buttons to be affixed to or set on any wearing apparel, solid sleeve buttons and solid studs . . . seals, bottle tickets, shoe clasps, patch boxes, salt spoons, tea strainers, caddy ladles, buckles and pieces to garnish cabinets or knife cases or tea chests, bridles or stands or frames'. The general effect was to tax the new fashion for small pieces of silver, most of

Tea Party
Attributed to Richard
Collins (d. 1732).

which were already being produced in Birmingham.

Between 1790 and 1844 there were a whole group of Acts that related either to the everyday running of assay offices, or to specific provincial towns. Then in 1844 an Act of general interest was passed. For the first time it was made an offence to possess a piece of 'fraudulent' silver, without giving an adequate explanation. The only possible grounds for discharge were if the poor unfortunate who was caught in possession could provide either the name and address of the man who had made the piece, or at least the whereabouts of the person from whom he had purchased it.

The Act of 1844 carried a completely new offence, in addition to the changing of the law concerning fraudulent pieces. This concerned the alteration of, or adding to, pieces of already hallmarked silver, a practice which became common at the beginning of the Victorian era. The Act made it illegal to change the character, denomination, or use of a piece, or even to make a small addition that affected the weight of a piece by more than four ounces in every troy pound. Every piece so altered had to be completely re-assayed as if it were new. Pieces which had been changed by less than the four ounces in a troy pound still had to have the additions assayed and hallmarked. Any retailer found in possession of a piece that did not conform to the new law was liable to a fine of £10 per item. This legislation only applied to England.

The Gold and Silverwares Act of 1854 has one section that, although very mild at first glance, was to have far-reaching effects on future legislation and administration concerning the assay offices. The statutes that had set up the new assay offices at Birmingham, Sheffield, and Glasgow, and had changed the law relating to Edinburgh, had in each case given the assay office a monopoly over all plate that was made within a specified area. This was important if a new assay office was to remain solvent. The 1854 Act changed this. It empowered 'workers and dealers in gold and silver' to register their names and marks 'at any assay office or assay offices established by the law which they may select'. This meant that for the first time an Exeter silversmith could register his mark in Dublin and Edinburgh, or vice versa.

Between 1854 and 1890, when the duty was removed, only two interesting things occurred which affect the hallmarks. In 1876 it was directed that 'clocks, watches or any other article of metal impressed with any mark or stamp representing or in imitation of any legal British assay mark or stamp, or purporting by any mark or appearance to be of the manufacture of the United Kingdom should be destroyed or otherwise disposed of as the Commissioners of Customs should direct'. This legislation was due mainly to the large quantity of plate in English styles with imitation hallmarks that was being brought into the country by people returning from the East, in particular India and China. In 1883 it was directed for the first time that all gold and silver plate imported into the United Kingdom was to be placed under bond until it had been to the assay office nearest the port of importation and assayed and marked. Pieces that were of substandard metal were returned unharmed to the importer, so long as he re-exported them within one month.

The legislation relating to imported goods was altered slightly in 1904. Then a new set of distinguishing marks were introduced to replace the 'F' mark that had been struck in addition to the regular hallmarks.

The new marks were to show the town of assay and

the quality of the metal from which the foreign goods were made, hence the standard (either .925 or .9584), in an oval punch, and an additional new distinguishing town mark (see tables). In 1907, the provision that imported plate should be assayed at the office nearest its place of importation was changed to the office of the importer's choice.

It was not until 1939 that the law concerning imported foreign goods was altered to differentiate between modern and second-hand goods and those which were antique; any piece 'which is proved to the satisfaction of the Commissioners of Customs and Excise to have been manufactured outside the United Kingdom more than 100 years before the year of importation' did not have to be assayed and hallmarked.

Thus a system of hallmarking has evolved over a period of some seven hundred years. For four hundred years apart from technical details, it has remained almost unchanged. The primary purpose of the system today is exactly the same as it was in the fourteenth century – to protect the customers.

*A 17th century
silversmith's workshop
from a pen and ink
drawing in Goldsmiths'
Hall.*

THE PROVINCES

ENGLAND

The Statute of 1423 granted 'divers touches' to seven English towns: Bristol, Coventry, Lincoln, Newcastle-upon-Tyne, Norwich, Salisbury, and York. Chester, which is known to have had a 'brotherhood' of goldsmiths at least from the early thirteenth century is omitted, possibly because it was seen to come under the control of the Earl of Chester. It is not easy to find anything in common between these towns. The most likely reason for their choice is that they were important in their area at that date, and in one way or another centres of communication. This made it easy for plate to be brought to them for assay from the surrounding countryside.

These towns continued to operate alongside a number of smaller towns whose guilds and smiths had developed their own system of marking until the introduction of the Britannia standard in 1696. After that, provincial assaying seems suddenly to have come to a halt, possibly because the local smiths had been recruited to work in the mints that were established to produce the 'new coinage', and to make the quick and efficient changeover by both increasing the production and spreading the distribution through the country.

To remedy this, the Plate Assay Act of 1700 was enacted which set up assay offices in Bristol, Chester, Exeter, Norwich, and York where mints had been started in 1696. The Act omitted Newcastle-upon-Tyne, but after representations from the smiths of that town the position was rectified in 1702. Of these five towns neither Bristol nor Norwich appear to have sustained an assay office, while the other towns took a civic symbol as their identifying mark or 'town mark'. Probably for the same reason as Bristol and Norwich – lack of working silversmiths – York closed its assay office in 1717, leaving only Chester, Exeter, and Newcastle, apart from London. In 1721, with the return to the old sterling standard, these three offices all reintroduced a leopard's head together with the lion passant (to replace the Britannia symbols), alongside the town mark, maker's mark, and date letter.

One of the fiercest political battles ever fought by the Goldsmiths' Company started in 1772. This concerned the proposition, supported by many important and influential goldsmiths and civic leaders, to open two new assay offices at Birmingham and Sheffield. Until then, the workers there were faced with the dangerous problem of sending wares on long journeys to assay towns to be tested and marked, without any guarantee that the marked goods would be sufficiently well wrapped to complete the return journey unharmed.

Two committees were established by Parliament to examine the proposition. They were petitioned by the London Goldsmiths' Company to reject the proposals, on the grounds that the general standard of silver would be threatened, and that as neither of these two towns had its own Goldsmiths' Guild, there would be no official body to protect the trade from malpractices. Despite the opposition from London the two assay offices were opened in 1773, apparently taking their marks not from their own town arms as had been traditional, but from the public house in the Strand – The Crown and Anchor – in which much of the lobbying had been done prior to the passing of the bill legalising their establishment. Sheffield adopted the crown; and Birmingham, the anchor. A few years later the assay office at York was re-opened.

During the following 80 years there was little change in English provincial assay offices. It became exceptional for a goldsmith not to send his wares to the nearest assay office, regardless of the magnitude or insignificance of the piece. This was mainly due to the stricter enforcement of the hallmarking laws, and a general improvement in the communication of those laws.

With the shifting of population from the rural districts to the new industrial towns in the first quarter of the nineteenth century, the smaller assay offices found the demand for their services falling. Local goldsmiths either retired without being replaced, or left for the glamour and increased prosperity of town life. One result of this exodus was that by 1880 the revenue from assay at both Exeter and Newcastle was insufficient to cover the cost of running the office; thus in 1882 the office at Exeter was closed, followed two years later by Newcastle. The reason for closure at York was not lack of business. The assay office there only really received work from one workshop from its re-opening in 1776 until it was closed after an enquiry into the way it was run in 1856.

Chester continued to assay and mark silver until 1962 when, in agreement with the recommendations of the Departmental Committee on Hallmarking, the office was closed. It is interesting that in the years preceding its closure over 90 per cent of the work tried at Chester was manufactured in Birmingham.

The remaining offices – those in Birmingham, London, and Sheffield – are all kept busy enough today to justify their remaining open. If anything, the modern trend is towards more new silver rather than less. For the Silver Jubilee of King George V in 1935 various manufacturers sold sets of teaspoons, each one marked at a different assay office and struck with a special punch with the joint heads of the King and Queen Mary.

CHESTER

Although there had been goldsmiths making money in Chester from Roman times it was not until about 1200 that the Earl Randle confirmed the establishment by charter of the 'guild merchant' in Chester. This almost certainly included the craft of goldsmith. The charter was in keeping with the main characteristic of Chester in that it came from the noble responsible for controlling the Palatine County, and not from the crown. It was in 1237 that the title Earl of Chester first gained a true authority for control of the county. The title was one of those taken by the heir to the throne. Chester, the capital city of the county, looked to him for protection and guidance concerning trade.

Like their brothers in the rest of England, the goldsmiths of Chester took a leading rôle in the civic affairs of the town throughout the mediaeval period. Many, such as John Dedwode, who was Sheriff in 1481, held high office. Their early history is very simple. The few goldsmiths conformed to their own guild rules, and even adopted the protection given to them by the Statute of 1300 though they did not seem to have sent anyone to London to collect their 'true touch'. Perhaps this was a reflection of their feeling of independence. From the end of the fourteenth century the importance of the goldsmiths in Chester began to wane. For a period of almost a hundred years civil war did not encourage patrons, even ecclesiastical ones. This was followed by the dissolution of the monasteries, which meant that for some years there were just the few orders to refashion surviving plate into something more fitting to the new order. It was not for some years that the fashion for large services of secular plate arrived from London. The local landowners who had prospered from the confiscated monastic lands and chantries became patrons of the craft.

The period of little work during the middle of the sixteenth century had led many of the goldsmiths to take up secondary occupations, as small farmers or tavern keepers. Lack of practice led to a deterioration in the quality of their work. In 1573 Chester was visited by two London goldsmiths, working for themselves as well as for the London Goldsmiths' company as 'supervisors of all the goldsmiths of England', a rôle given to them in 1461. These London smiths were efficient in their task of trying local plate, which appears not to have needed to be assayed at this period. The goldsmith had to put his mark on every piece so that if it was found to be substandard at a later date he could be suitably punished. Smiths whose work was found to be substandard were fined and charged for making their oath in Nantwich. The goldsmiths would not co-operate within the city since they could hide behind the city charter given by Henry VII.

During the last 30 years of the sixteenth century the Chester goldsmiths seem to have prospered. They made new plate for the surrounding parishes and most of the parishes in Northern Wales as well as secular plate for the surrounding great houses. One man, William Mutton, emerged as the leader of the revival. He was Sheriff for a short time and produced what must be a considerable number of items, judging from the amount of surviving plate. Unfortunately, the beginning of the seventeenth century seems to have heralded a depression for the Chester goldsmiths. The leading families just managed to continue but without any great quantity of orders or signs of encouragement. This may have been due to the sudden improvement in communications that followed the road-building of the end of the six-teenth century, further encouraging prospective patrons to order what was considered 'finer' plate from London rather than from their local goldsmiths.

One result of the civil war, during which Chester was passionately pro-Royalist, was the seizure during two different sieges of much of the available plate for the payment of the King's army. The effect of the war on Chester silversmiths was to further diminish their prosperity. Even by 1660 and the Restoration of the monarchy, it was still some years before there was any sign of a revival of the craft. Eventually, silver was once more in demand, silversmithing once more a profitable pursuit, and the Chester Goldsmiths once more a viable company.

In exact opposition to the policy of the previous years, when it had been necessary for both impoverished Parliament, Crown, and the landowners to melt plate to make coin, the new era of affluence led to melting of coin to make plate, culminating in 1697 with the new coinage and introduction of the Britannia standard. Before the introduction of the Britannia standard and since 1686, the goldsmiths had sorted out a regular system of assay – a system of date letters and an assay mark of the old town Coat of Arms. This was dropped in 1697 with the introduction of the new Act. Many of the makers reverted to the older practice of striking a piece with their own mark only, or even their own mark and the word 'sterling', rather than continue with the previous system. (The word sterling has also been used in Cork and Limerick in Ireland as well as Liverpool at the beginning of the eighteenth century and Sheffield c. 1770.)

The Act of 1701 reinstated the provincial assay offices

that had been open before 1697, with the exception of Newcastle and with the addition of Exeter. Newcastle was added the following year. The Act introduced the need for goldsmiths to strike their mark on a copper plate and keep a full minute book of each one of their meetings.

Throughout the eighteenth century the makers who had greatest effect on the progress of silversmithing in Chester were the Richardson family, whose influence extended throughout the century. Not only were they fine craftsmen and good businessmen, but they exerted a strong influence to keep the Goldsmiths' Company of Chester together and to encourage the trade. The principal produce of this prolific family, apart from flatware, was tumbler cups in the middle of the century, and skewers towards the end. All of these are scarce in comparison with the products of other provincial towns such as Exeter and Newcastle.

The use of a crowned leopard's head from 1719, continued until about 1820 when an uncrowned leopard was introduced. The leopard's head was used on its own for the following 20 years. However, it did not look like a British hallmark and was later discontinued.

The quantity of plate made in Chester steadily declined during the nineteenth century although, as had been the practice from the end of the eighteenth century, much was sent from Birmingham, especially by manufacturers anxious to preserve the secrecy of a new design. Towards the end of the century, Chester, the nearest port to Liverpool, was responsible for the assay of large quantities of imported plate in addition to Birmingham work. The office continued until 1962 when it was closed as the result of a government report which found that it was not sufficiently busy.

*York 6d token of 1811
issued by silversmiths
Robert Cattle and James
Barber, showing town
coat of arms.*

47

YORK

York was by far the most important of the English cities of the Middle Ages, and was known to have had a 'goldsmith's craft' as early as the thirteenth century. In 1432 it was known to have a mark or touch. This was probably the one mentioned in legislation in the Act of 1300. There was a dispute between local members of the craft as to whether there should be two or three officials appointed to 'search the trade' and mark all pieces found to be of the proper standard with the 'common touch of the said city'. It is interesting that a silversmith in the city could not submit a piece for assay, or try to sell it, unless it bore his own identifying mark. The penalty was the large sum of 6s 8d (33p).

The Act of 1423 which reaffirmed the sterling standard stated that the mentioned towns, of which York was one, were to set up as assay towns, each having divers touches 'to the ordinance of the mayors, bailiffs or governors of the same towns'. This was exactly the case in York where a 'touch ordained in the City of York according to the ordinance of its mayor' is recorded. This city at least conformed to the statute.

That there were many goldsmiths working at York during the fifteenth century is not surprising, because it was the centre of the North of England, not only of monastic life but for the wool trade. Even at this time much money meant much plate, especially from the now huge monasteries. Much of this plate must have been destroyed in the years of the dissolution. Little survives.

The records of the city of York are helpful in producing relevant information. Following the dispute over the number of searchers in 1410, there was an ordinance which instructs that 'all work should be touched with the pounce (punch) of this city, called the half leopard head and half fleur de lis'. Presumably this was a compromise with the instruction to use a leopard's head given in the Act of 1300.

Little is known of the fate of the goldsmiths of York during the early years of the sixteenth century, but it is safe to assume that their fortunes followed those of their brothers in the rest of the country – poor from the end of the monasteries until the new affluence of the Elizabethan age. There are some very amusing accounts in the records of the York Goldsmiths' Company including an entry relating the story of 'searchers', Martin du Biggin and William Pearson. Although their offence is not specifically mentioned it can be safely assumed to concern their task as goldsmith-searchers, especially as the punishment of Martin du Biggin was imprisonment at the pleasure of the Mayor.

Like other goldsmiths elsewhere, York smiths held many of the top civic posts during the Middle Ages. These included Lord Mayor or Sheriff even up to 1697, when Mark Gill was Lord Mayor. There was, as far as can be ascertained, a regular system of hallmarking in York as early as 1560. This continued without interruption through to 1697 when, in common with the other provincial offices, the company found itself denuded of working members and confused as to the exact interpretation of the law. The regular marking of plate then ceased.

This situation remained until the Plate Assay Act of 1700 which, for the first time, incorporated on the statute books as separate companies all the 'goldsmiths, silversmiths and plate workers who are or shall be freemen of and inhabiting within any of the said cities and having served an apprenticeship to the said trade'. In further pursuance of the Act the town mark was changed to a cross charged with five lions passant, the arms of the city. It would appear that the operation of the assay office was not sufficiently profitable to the York company. In 1717 it was discontinued. The leading makers, Joseph Buckle and John Langwith, had to petition Newcastle to have their plate assayed there for an agreed annual fee.

Between 1717 and the re-opening of the office in 1776 no plate at all appears to have been assayed in York. All plate that was made there was sent to Newcastle for this purpose.

The revival of hallmarking at York was mainly the result of the work of the partnership, John Hampston and John Prince. Their firm in different forms remained the only producer of any importance during the whole period up to 1857 while the assay office was open. It is probable that the firm of Hampston and Prince was not only responsible for the production of most of the plate that was assayed but for the making of the punches with which it was struck. On small pieces, made between 1793 and 1811, it is common to find the lion passant of the mark struck facing in the wrong direction. This is not the only peculiarity concerning the marks; the third cycle of letters, using the 'k' for three years, missing out the 'l' and 'm' altogether.

The marks actually used by the office were often of a curious nature. The town mark was reserved for larger pieces and only *very* rarely appeared on anything as small as flatware. This can lead to confusion with London marks. The simplest way to tell the difference is that while the York leopard's head is always in a shield with four right-angled corners, this is never the case with the leopard's heads used in London between 1776 and 1858. There was much irregularity both in the use of the marks and running of the assay office which, combined with a reduction in the number of pieces led to the closure of the office in 1858.

Many of the larger pieces made during this later period and bearing York makers' marks were not made in York at all, but by leading London goldsmiths who sold them unmarked to the York maker. He then submitted them for assay and marked them as his own wares.

EXETER

The craft of goldsmithing at Exeter is probably at least as old as that of York and Chester despite the fact that there appears to be no official acknowledgement of the craft's existence before the Plate Assay Act of 1701. The reason for this omission is difficult to understand because from the large quantity of extant mediaeval plate made in Exeter still surviving, in comparison with that made in the 'assay' towns, it is apparent that there was an active guild of craftsmen there.

A guild of Exeter goldsmiths was recorded during the fifteenth century. It is probable that there had been one there for the best part of 200 years. Towards the end of the fourteenth century a certain John de Welinworth was recorded. It seems from contemporary documents that he was a man of some importance in the district as well as an active goldsmith. It is even more confusing that there is no mention of Exeter in the Act of 1423. This Act specifically mentions both Bristol and Salisbury, two towns that appear to have produced much less plate than Exeter.

During the sixteenth century, goldsmithing in Exeter appears to have fared in common with the rest of the country except that its revival from about 1570 was much more marked. During this period there were some

51

Covered tankard made in Exeter in 1701 by John Elston with close-up of marks on the lid.

half dozen smiths working in Exeter, producing plate for the many surrounding parishes as well as the local nobility. The most important of these was John Johns, who was responsible for producing some very fine work.

Exeter, like many of the larger provincial towns, was under siege during the civil war. Much of the civic, though little of the ecclesiastical, plate was reduced to coin to pay troops. Exeter's trade does not seem to have been as badly hit as it was elsewhere in the years immediately following the civil war. This was perhaps due to the strong pro-Royalist and at the same time anti-Catholic population who were not so badly affected by the austerity demanded by the puritanical central government.

In the years preceding 1697 it would appear that the craft continued without much expansion – by now there was much competition from the surrounding towns and villages notably Barnstaple, Truro, Taunton, and Plymouth. All had their own groups of smiths. It is not clear whether there was any activity between 1697 and 1701 when an assay office was officially opened in Exeter for the first time by statute. As in other provincial towns it is unlikely that work would have suddenly come to an end, but more reasonable to assume that the system of marking formerly in use was abandoned.

In August 1701, 11 Exeter goldsmiths met to discuss the setting up of an assay office. A month later the first two wardens were elected. Once the new office was seen to be in full use the Exeter goldsmiths felt secure enough to notify the goldsmiths working in surrounding towns that the office was now ready, and prepared to assay plate in accordance with the Act of 1700. The response appears to have been good. Many makers registered their marks and came from such towns as Dartmouth.

Because the Act of 1700 directed that the town mark should be a representation of the town Coat of Arms, the Exeter goldsmiths had to stop using the mark of a crowned X and replace it with a punch showing a three towered castle. This mark was used in various forms up to the closure of the office in 1882. The other marks used in the first cycle, up to 1719, are the figure of Britannia, a lion's head erased, date letter, and maker's mark. In 1720, rather than have new punches made at some expense, the assay office merely altered the Britannia mark to a lion passant and the lion's head erased to that of a leopard's head. This means that for the following few years the marks on sterling standard wares sometimes appear to carry Britannia symbols.

In 1773 a government committee was set up, as the result of the proposed legislation concerning new assay offices at Birmingham and Sheffield, to enquire into the manner in which the provincial assay offices were run. The report from Mr. Matthew Skinner, assay master at Exeter is quite revealing. Mr. Skinner stated that although he took oath on taking office it was not the official oath and he had never taken instruction from anybody on how to make an assay, but taught himself by experiment. He had never assayed a piece of gold in his life. He went on 'that the standard for Plate is 11oz 2dwt of fine silver and 18dwt of alloy; but I allow a remedy of 2dwt in the pound because it would be hard upon a working tradesman if he was not allowed something as he does his best . . .'

The same document (1773) stated that there were only five members of the Goldsmiths' Company of Exeter, two of whom had not finished their apprenticeships, and one of them, Matthew Skinner, had been assay master since 1757. There were some 15 other makers who had marks registered and their wares tried there. Most came from Plymouth. In 1777 the leopard's head punch was struck for the last time, thus reducing the number of marks being used by one for the next seven years.

Apart from one slight irregularity – that much of the plate assayed in 1786 showed the old duty mark of an intaglio king's head – there is nothing particularly unusual about the marks and history of the Exeter goldsmiths until about 1812. At this date a smith called George Ferris first appears. This man was the only Exeter smith of the period to run a workshop. In a period of some 20 years, he made a large number of quite important pieces of plate. The nineteenth century, though, saw the decline of provincial assay offices and makers with the exception of the two new centres of cheaper and more reliable work, Birmingham and Sheffield. This decline continued until in 1880 the income from assaying was insufficient to cover the cost of maintaining the assay office and it was shut in 1882.

NEWCASTLE

Very little is known of the early history of the Newcastle goldsmiths. There is little positive evidence of their existence before 1300, and no mention in statute until 1423. Then Newcastle was one of the towns set up as an assay town, having a touch 'according to the ordinance of the Mayor, Bailiff or Governor'. It would appear that the goldsmiths took no notice of this ordinance for three years. By special ordinance the bailiffs were instructed to find 'two fit and prudent goldsmiths to be assayers of the money'. This seems to point to the fact that there was not already a system of assay in the town.

Little is known of the activities of the Newcastle goldsmiths during the fifteenth century, but in 1536 the goldsmiths, glaziers, plumbers, pewterers, and painters of Newcastle became an incorporation of trades for their own protection. The charter, a fascinating document, was given by the Mayor, Sheriff, and aldermen of the city and laid down strict rules for the running of the company. It was to be run by a committee of four wardens of different trades. No member was permitted to practise another trade at risk of a heavy fine (3s 4d or 17p).

The company was anti-Scots. It was a serious offence for a member to take 'a Scots man borne in Scotland' and employ him as a journeyman or even take him on as an apprentice. For this the fine was 40s (£2.00), half of which was for the benefit of the company, the other half for the maintainance and upkeep of the bridge over the Tyne. The degree to which the members of the company disliked the Scots cannot be better shown than by the punishment given to any member of the company who dared to call another member 'a Scot, a murderer and a thief': the poor miscreant, once found guilty, was thrown out of the company for as long as the company so wished, and had to pay a re-entrance fee when he was eventually allowed to rejoin.

Although the number of goldsmiths recorded in the minutes of the company for the middle and end of the sixteenth century is surprisingly large, there is practically no work still in existence from that period. This is puzzling, but the lack of work from the first quarter of the seventeenth century can be explained. As there were no goldsmith members of the company, work presumably needed to be brought from London or York. The lack of goldsmiths continued well into the Protectorate of Oliver Cromwell during which one William Ramsey joined the company as its only goldsmith. This heralded a revival. About a dozen other goldsmiths became members, including William Ramsey's son.

Like all other provincial manufacturers, the goldsmiths of Newcastle found themselves in a dilemma over the interpretation of the 1697 Act. As a result, there is very little marked plate that can definitely be ascribed to the four years following the Act. The Act of 1700 re-established Exeter and Chester as assay towns. Newcastle was omitted from the Act as it did not have a mint for helping to produce and distribute the new coinage. So hurt were the Newcastle goldsmiths that they petitioned the House of Commons for an assay office. Their plea was backed by a similar petition from the Mayor, aldermen, and common council of the town, laying out the reasons why they thought that they would be most likely to influence Parliament, 'whereas in the town of Newcastle-upon-Tyne there is and time out of mind hath been an ancient company of goldsmiths which, with their families are like to be ruined and their trade utterly lost in that said town . . . they being in danger of losing the greater part of their trade which chiefly consists of plate bespoke to be wrought up in a short time, and they cannot have it returned from York in less than a fortnight's time'. Parliament took notice of these petitions and in 1702 passed a special Act which re-established the assay office at Newcastle.

The marks that they were required to use were the same as the other provincial assay towns; the lion's head erased, the figure of Britannia, and the arms of the city, namely three castles. The Goldsmiths' Company remained a part of the incorporated trade until 1716. After that date it split away, held its own meetings and kept its own minute books. The Newcastle goldsmiths, like their brothers at York and Chester, kept a copper plate on which was struck the maker's mark of everyone who registered at the assay office. The Newcastle copper plate is struck with some 300 marks dating from 1702 to 1880.

In response to the committee of enquiry of 1773, the Newcastle company was found to have 10 members. One came from Durham and one from Sunderland. It states that the amount of plate assayed in Newcastle over a five year period, 1769 to 1772, was over 55 per cent more than that assayed at Exeter. Even allowing for the plate assayed in Chester from 1770 to 1772, it was over 10,000 ounces a year more. The quantities of plate tried at Chester before 1770 were truly tiny – only 161 ounces in 1769, as opposed to Newcastle's 10,987. Indeed, in this year more plate was broken at Newcastle for being of substandard quality than was assayed correct at Chester.

There was an amusing episode in 1844 when a Bill was put before Parliament that would give the London Goldsmiths' Company the right, should it find any substandard but marked provincial wares, to sue the assay office in question. The outcome of this was much lobbying on behalf of the provincial goldsmiths, not least those of Newcastle, to have the Act amended. Eventually it was, much to the annoyance of the London Company, who were now themselves liable to be sued should any of their marked wares turn out to be substandard.

In keeping with the rest of the country, the improvement in communications and advantages of the factories of Sheffield and Birmingham had an adverse effect on the demand for plate in Newcastle. Eventually it had to close in 1884.

SHEFFIELD

Although it was only in the second half of the eighteenth

Queen Anne tea kettle and stand made in 1708 in London by David Willaume.

century that Sheffield became a town of any importance, it had already gained a good reputation for the production of iron work before then. The discovery of steel as a working material and the sudden increase in the number of mass produced goods in the 1760s established Sheffield as the centre of the country's steel production. Steel had been used for over a century for knife blades. For the first time it was possible to produce resin-filled silver handles very cheaply with die-stamping machines. So successful were they that the Sheffield manufacturers began to turn their die-stamping methods to other pieces of silver, such as pierced baskets, candle sticks, and many others.

Consequently, a petition was presented to Parliament, stating that the silversmiths and plate workers of Sheffield were working under great difficulties and hardship in the exercise of their trades, for want of assayers in convenient places to assay and mark their plate. The situation had indeed been so extreme that in the three years preceding the petition it had been common for the individual makers to strike the word 'sterling' in addition to their maker's mark on a finished piece before setting it to sale, rather than go to the bother of sending it to be assayed.

The petition met with fierce resistance from the London Goldsmiths' Company who produced a variety of reasons objecting to the establishment of any new assay offices, mainly based on the excuse that the new office might not properly exercise its purpose and mark substandard plate. Despite the objection, the Act was passed. The Act was the first attempt to establish a code to regulate the privileges, powers, obligations, and management of an assay office. It gave the names of 30 people whom it incorporated as a Company for Sheffield to be known as the 'Guardians of the wrought plate of the town of Sheffield', and provided that four wardens should be elected each year, each of whom had to live within a 20-mile radius of the city. The same 20-mile radius was used in the legislation – all goldsmiths, silversmiths, and plateworkers within the area were forbidden by law to sell any manufacture made there unless it had first been tried and marked appropriately.

The office opened in 1773, strangely starting with the date letter E, though perhaps this was due to the fact that one of the Sheffield makers' champions, the president of their company was the Earl of Effingham. From its opening the office was only available for the taking in and assaying of plate on two days a week, until the quantity of plate became so great that the hours had to be extended. From 1780 it was decided that as a number of very small, though dutiable items were being submitted for assay, there should be a punch available which incorporated the town mark and date letter in case there was not room for the two to be struck separately on a piece. This practice was unique to the Sheffield office.

Sheffield was one of the towns that profited by the Act of 1854 which allowed smiths to register their marks and send their wares to be assayed at any assay office of their choice. The previous monopoly of their home town had often led to a practice of re-marking at other provincial offices when a local smith had bought Sheffield wares for retail sale. This was common in Edinburgh.

The Plate Assay (Sheffield) Act, apart from increasing the amounts that could be charged for assay, made it lawful: 'for any manufacturer of goods plated with silver within Sheffield or within 100 miles thereof (this radius including Birmingham!) to strike his or her surname or other name or firm', with a warning that the mark must not be in imitation of any hallmark. As an additional precaution, the act continued: 'and every such mark figure or device shall before the same is made use of be submitted to the examination of the said Company of Guardians'. The guardians were bound to keep a book into which they would enter all plate marks so submitted on payment from the manufacturer of a registration mark of 2s 6d (12½p). The penalty for the manufacturer of striking a mark he hadn't first registered at the assay office was £100.

BIRMINGHAM

The establishment of an assay office at Sheffield was concurrent with that of Birmingham. The two were set up with the same strict rules under the Act of Parliament, although the town of Birmingham had 36 directed members of its new company compared with Sheffield which had 30. The establishment of Birmingham as an assay office at all was probably largely due to the efforts of one man, Matthew Boulton, whose common sense and business acumen had by 1771 established a large and prosperous business in Birmingham making cast steel and Sheffield plate as well as silver. There was no easy place for Boulton to send his products to be assayed, for, unlike the ever-growing number of manufacturers producing small pieces in the town, his goods would not pack into small cases for easy transport. Boulton's eagerness for the establishment of an assay office can be illustrated by a letter he sent to his partner, James Fothergill in May 1773. He mentioned his attempts to bribe ministers to speed up the passing of the Act by giving them steel sword-hilts. He even boasted that on seeing Lord Denbeigh's the King had asked for one!

The progress of Birmingham as an assay office was encouraged by the boom of small makers towards the end of the eighteenth century; small pieces of silver were now fashionable – vinaigrettes, patch boxes, travelling cases, toilet boxes, buckles – the list is endless, but by far the majority of these small pieces were made and assayed in Birmingham.

Apart from the removal of its area monopoly in 1854, and after the disastrous change of fashion that put most of the buckle-makers out of work, there was very little of note that concerned the Birmingham office. Its main task was manufacturing wares.

BRISTOL AND NORWICH

Despite frequent mentions in legislation, neither Bristol nor Norwich appear to have had very busy assay offices, or even goldsmiths' companies, after the late Middle Ages, apart from a late revival by Norwich toward the end of the seventeenth century. It is apparent that Norwich was the centre of a very large silversmithing craft throughout the fourteenth and fifteenth centuries. A large number who are known to have worked there are recorded from as early as 1285. It is apparent that there was a flourishing, but much smaller, craft of goldsmiths still working during the Elizabethan period. The plate made by them is usually of a superlative quality. It often surpasses London pieces of the same period – not only in quality of workmanship but in design.

In a document dated 1564 the goldsmiths of Norwich admit that the 'touch' granted to them under the Statute of 1423 had never been introduced. This led to mis-application of their talents by individual goldsmiths. But the situation was apparently set right and an official system of hallmarking started in 1565 that was to continue until the Act of 1697. The town mark used was that of the city arms – a lion passant surmounted by a castle. This mark was also adopted for the short life of the office after it was officially allowed to re-open in 1701, after consultation by post at least twice with the goldsmiths' company of Chester.

During the seventeenth century a great deal of plate was made in Norwich, serving the whole of East Anglia. Much of it had a distinctive design, probably due to the influence of the Dutch colony that resided just outside the town. The presence of this colony had an effect on the whole life of the city, including the architecture and plumbing methods. It may be, too, that because of the colony's slightly unstable population, the Norwich company devised the simple oath that had to be sworn by all 'foreigners or immigrant silversmiths'. Foreigners in this instance meant English goldsmiths who were either members of a different company, or not members of any company.

Bristol, like Norwich, is mentioned in the Act of 1423, but it is difficult to establish the continuance and prosperity of the craft between that date and 1697 because of the distinct lack of any form of contemporary records. That it was mentioned in the Act of 1701 does not in itself mean much, because Norwich, which only used its re-established privilege for two years, was also mentioned in the same Act. There are, however, a rare set of marks that would appear to belong to a second series of date letters (starting, say, in 1725) bearing a punch which clearly carries the arms of the city of Bristol – a ship issuing from a castle – but pieces with this mark, together with lion passant and leopard's head crowned, letter A or B, and maker's mark, are so scarce as to be confusing.

It should be noted that Bristol, Norwich and York appear in the terms of reference for the committee of enquiry in 1773. The committee reports that 'London, Chester, Exeter and Newcastle-upon-Tyne (being the only assay offices which they find are now kept up in this kingdom) . ⁀ .' which is the only official confirmation of the new function of these offices.

SCOTLAND

The history of the Scottish goldsmiths, their craft, and assay offices is different from that of the English smiths, primarily because of the scattered distribution of the relatively small population. The Scottish goldsmiths developed independently of their English neighbours, almost it seems in deliberate contrast. While the style of the English wares was quite distinct from those of the continent, the Scottish wares were often almost indistinguishable from the pieces made at the same time by their main trading partners, Holland and France.

There must have been a fair demand for silver from the many monasteries of Scotland, despite the fact that some had their own goldsmiths and others belonged to the 'reformed' orders. They made a virtue out of not having too much plate, were very wealthy and extracted the maximum profit from their not insignificant holdings of land. An example of the sort of holding of plate that they might be expected to have held is the inventory of the jewels and plate at the Abbey of Coupar in 1296. But the many chalices, spoons, cups and silver dishes and even salt cellars were later to be broken up by order of the king and renewed by a London goldsmith. It is difficult to estimate how much secular silversmithing was carried out in Scotland before the start of the seventeenth century. Little survives. There are many

London 1813

Exeter 1806 by Joseph Hicks

Newcastle 1757 by John Langlands – John Robertson

Chester 1814 by John Sutters

Birmingham 1816 by Joseph Willmore

Edinburgh 1827

Platinum mark as introduced on 1 January 1975

66

reasons for this, not least the vigour of the mid-sixteenth century reformers and the mobs that followed them.

About 1300 ounces of the silver that had belonged to Mary Queen of Scots was melted for coinage. The same thing happened to the 333 ounce gold font that had been the present of Elizabeth I of England for the baptism of the infant James VI (later James I of England).

Laws for hallmarking in Scotland began in 1457, under James II when a statute was enacted 'to eschew the deceiving done to the Kings Lieges'. The Act was devised to discourage a common practice of adding impurities to the silver brought in by a customer for re-fashion to increase the profit. It is clear from the phrasing of the Act that there were a large number of working goldsmiths at this time. But all except the largest towns were not organised. The Act appoints 'a cunning man of gude conscience quhick sall be Deakone of the craft' who, having tried a piece was, as an additional safeguard for the customer to place his mark alongside that of the maker if he found it to be of acceptable standard.

The standard required, as set out in the Act was different for both gold and silver from that required of the English smiths. The required standard for gold was 20 carats (20 grains of pure gold in every 24); for silver XI grains fine – which is 11 ounces of pure silver in every 12 ounces troy, or 916.6 parts per thousand. Unlike England, provision was made for towns with only one goldsmith. He could take his work to the 'head offices of the town' who were responsible for placing a mark indicating the name of the town near to the maker's mark. This legislation, although apparently foolproof was still open to abuse. To reduce the number of malpractices, a follow-up statute was introduced 26 years later. This attempted to undo the harm done to the trade

67

by some goldsmiths 'myning too much laye with their silver'. It was made compulsory for each town with a goldsmith or smiths to appoint a warden or a deacon to test all the silver produced in that town. They had to put their marks jointly on every piece that was found up to standard (the modern phrase 'up to scratch' is derived from the scratching of silver in order to make an assay), while confiscating every piece that was found to be substandard.

The year 1483 sees yet more legislation, mainly re-phrasing that of the two previous Acts, but with certain additions. The most important is probably the acknow-ledgement of the existence of the members of the craft as a body. It states that, 'no goldsmith was to be a master nor is he to hold "open booth" (sell in public) unless he shall be admitted by the officer of the craft and the whole body of it'. In this same year the Edinburgh hammermen, a group of all the smithing crafts, but usually led by the 'senior' craft of goldsmith, required of its members that 'al goldsmytis werk be markit wt his avn mark, the dekynis mark, and the mark of the tovne, of the finance of a 11d fine'. This may have been necessary because the smiths in the town did not take heed of the legislation concerning their work.

There is little change in the law between 1485 and 1555 except the introduction of the standard of Bruges in 1489. This was not a stable standard. At its worst it was 917 per 1000 pure for small work. From at least 1515 the standard for large pieces was the surprisingly high figure of 946 parts per 1000. The standard stated that when a piece of silver was taken to a smith to be re-fashioned it had to be assayed before it was melted, an unprecedented requirement. The test of its authenticity was whether, after being refashioned, it assayed the same as originally. The Smith was liable to a large fine if it turned out to be of a worse purity.

The standard of Bruges was enforced until 1555 when the next Statute of any importance was enacted, which had a long preamble concerning 'the great fraud and hurt done unto the lieges of the realme by goldsmiths that make silver and gold of no certain finesse'. The standard for gold was changed by the Act to 22 carats. This was 20 years before the English reached this higher standard. At the same time the old 'Scots' standard of 916.6, mentioned in the Act of 1457, was restored. The probable reason for the apparent lowering of the standard and abandonment of the standard of Bruges is that the twin standards made possible under this latter were the cause of confusion and dispute between the goldsmiths and their deacons.

In 1586 the deacon and master of the goldsmiths craft (guild) were granted their first Letters Patent, a charter which gave the goldsmiths of Edinburgh the same power in Scotland as that held by the London Goldsmiths' Company, south of the border. This appears to be the first time that the Edinburgh goldsmiths are acknowledged as an entity in themselves as opposed to members of the city's Corporation of Hammermen. The Edinburgh goldsmiths seem to have adopted the castle as their mark toward the beginning of the sixteenth century and to have been strict in the supervision of their craft. Not long after the granting of the charter they fined or confiscated plate from a great number of the local smiths.

The progress of silversmithing in Scotland suffered a shattering blow from the Reformation. Not only were the fine ecclesiastical patrons removed, but they were replaced by an order so impoverished that its ministers were often reduced to selling ale to the parishioners to maintain themselves. Unlike England, secular patrons of the goldsmiths didn't become more prosperous after the Reformation. It is surprising that so many relatively large pieces yet few smaller examples remain from this period.

In 1681 the Edinburgh goldsmiths added a date letter to their other marks. From that date it was possible to place a piece at an exact year rather than the period during which a particular deacon held office. Four years later James VII (James II of England) granted a new charter to the Edinburgh goldsmiths to confirm their privileges and extend their powers to punish offenders against the hallmarking laws. As the result, the Edinburgh smiths wrote to the other towns that they knew had working goldsmiths to direct their attention to the importance of keeping their gold and silver work up to standard. The towns included Aberdeen, Ayr, Banff, Glasgow, Inverness, Montrose and Perth.

The 1707 Act of Union provided for the law relating to hallmarking 'to remain in the same force as before . . . but they to be alterable by the Parliament of Great Britain'. This ruling disconcerted the Scottish goldsmiths.

In 1719 when the Britannia standard became optional and a duty of sixpence an ounce was introduced, the English goldsmiths were allowed to use less fine and thus less expensive plate in exchange for the burden of the new tax. In Scotland, however, where the Britannia had never been used, the effect of the first measure was nil. The effect of the second bordered on disaster. To compensate for the new duty the smiths had to raise the price of their plate and as a result there was a significant drop in demand.

Most of the Acts passed through the rest of the

eighteenth century applied only to England. Those that applied to Scotland affected the duty on plate. During this period the Edinburgh goldsmiths reached their peak in many ways and surpassed the reliability of their London cousins with the quality of work. They were the elite of the city's merchant classes, yet still worker-craftsmen. They traded with all levels of society: from the rich and extravagant nobility to country couples anxious to gain a set of teaspoons for their wedding. There is a revealing mention in the day-book of James Beattie for 13 April 1782: 'Paid to John Davidson, Goldsmith for six teaspoons and a sugar spoon – marked (engraved with the initials) J.B. – £1 9s 0d (£1-45p)'. It is interesting that it was fashionable at this time for the final payment and collection of pieces ordered on earlier visits to be made in one of the nearby coffee houses. It is not uncommon to find in contemporary accounts the purchaser adding the cost of the coffee or spirit to the cost of his acquisitions.

The Statute of 1819 was the first to impinge on the right of the Edinburgh goldsmiths to instruct the craft in the rest of the country. This Act names 27 people, all 'gold and silversmiths and plateworkers' who it incorporated into a company to be known as 'The Glasgow Goldsmiths' Company'. The 27 were appointed for life on the condition that they should continue to live in Glasgow, or within a 40-mile radius, south and west. They were instructed to elect four wardens who lived either in the city or in a radius of 10 miles to the south and west who were to be re-elected once a year. The Act declared that no silversmith living within the 40-mile radius should sell any goods that had not been tried by the new assay office, whose standard of purity was 'sterling, or 925 parts pure silver in a thousand' and marked with a maker's mark, a lion rampant, the mark of the company (the city coat of arms) 'to denote the goodness thereof' and a variable date letter. The Act introduced the sterling standard for the first time in Scotland and the alternative Britannia standard, as allowed in England from 1720. The assay master for the new office was appointed for life unless he was found to have neglected his duty or was incapable due to ill health.

The 1819 Statute created an extraordinary and ambiguous situation. On one side of the country was Edinburgh which had been autonomous until this Statute and which required a minimum standard of 916.6, while less than 100 miles away on the other side of the country was the newly appointed office in Glasgow which required a minimum standard of 925. This led to the transference, even by the leading Glasgow goldsmiths, of much of the lower standard plate to Edinburgh, and the subsequent under-use of the Glasgow assay office. It was not until 1836 that this situation was rectified by the introduction of the sterling standard for the whole of the United Kingdom. From 1836 onward a great amount of plate was assayed at Glasgow. The Statute of 1836 also required that all work done in Scotland should be sent for assay to either Edinburgh or Glasgow.

Scotland, because of its small size, the relative remoteness of many of its townships and the great risk and long distances involved in transporting plate for assay, was unique in that nearly every 'burgh' had a smith. It was the rule rather than the exception for him to make the punches with which he marked a piece. The most important of these towns are: Aberdeen, Banff, Dumfries, Dundee, Elgin, Forress, Greenock, Inverness, Montrose,

One of a pair of beer jugs made in 1768 in London by Charles Wright.

Perth, Tain and Wick. A study of these towns, the history of their craftsmen and development of their marks is both absorbing and complex, but as their wares are scarce they are outside the scope of anything but a specialist work.

IRELAND

The history of the goldsmiths of Ireland can be traced back to pre-Norman times. Certainly there was much fine plate made there between then and the fifteenth century when by virtue of Poynings Law in 1495. The Plate Act of 1423 was retrospectively applied to English-ruled Ireland. But there is little evidence as to any effect that it might have had. Record of a petition from Dublin Goldsmiths' company to the city council in 1555 appears to have guaranteed their status since the previous charter had been 'accidentally burnt'. They were anxious that with the loss of the charter there might be an equivalent loss in the privileges they enjoyed. It was not until 1557 that the worried goldsmiths were granted their petition and allowed to operate their guild within the law again.

In 1605 as the result of both low standard plate sold in Dublin and the disappearance of a large volume of the civic plate which was suspected of finding its way into the melting pot of local goldsmiths, the city council took action. The council passed a resolution that each gold-smith should· have his own mark and that all plate put up for sale after 1 January 1606 should have first been assayed by the 'Mayor and constables' of the city. It was also declared that the standard for plate should be the same as for coin, namely sterling and that the mark of assay should be the figure of a 'lion, harp, and a castle'.

King Charles I granted a charter of incorporation to

the Dublin goldsmiths in 1637. Under this there were provisions for the regular assay and marking of plate that was made within their jurisdiction. To comply with the conditions of the charter the mark of a crowned harp was adopted to signify that the plate had been assayed and found to be of acceptable quality. Date letters were also introduced in 1638. These changed every year. The charter also gave the Dublin goldsmiths company the same rights and powers as the Goldsmiths' Company of London. One good result of the charter from an historical viewpoint is that from its date there is a more or less complete record of the proceedings of the Dublin Goldsmiths' Company. These were kept in the form of minute, account and note books. Nearly all were preserved. From these it is possible to gather some insight into the fortunes of the Dublin goldsmiths, and those of the goldsmiths of the whole of Britain over the next 90 years. There is an annual record of the total weight of all the items assayed in each year. The average drops from about 1300 ounces a year before 1644, the start of the civil war, to about 230 between 1644 and 1649. During that period the war was at its most destructive. The figure would have dropped even lower during the next seven years while Cromwell was in Ireland, but from 1657 there is a steady increase in the amount of business – 8500 ounces were assayed in that year. This trend led to the introduction of the Britannia standard and closing of the provincial assay offices in England. By 1700 the figure had risen to about 26000 ounces and by 1725 to 60000!! And this was despite the three years of war while James II of England was defending his throne against William of Orange. It is amusing in the light of history that in November 1691 the new assay master was delivered 'several pieces of plate that had been placed in custody by the corporation some time before the late troubles'.

There is ample evidence of the efficiency with which the company acted in its task of 'searching out bad plate that should be destroyed'. Records for the late seventeenth century are full of mentions of offenders and their fines. One persistent offender appears to have been a goldsmith, David Swan whose shop was searched by the assay master and wardens. They found some pieces of substandard plate. But David Swan opposed them in a 'contemptous and unworthy manner' by 'forcing back said cups (the substandard ones already located by the searchers) and putting them into his breeches pockets he ran into a room behind his shop and hid same in an obscure place'. He was later coerced into revealing where he had hidden the cups and fined. The cups were destroyed.

The Dublin goldsmiths appear to have had more than a fair share in the running of their own city. Many became sheriffs or aldermen. Daniel Bellingham, a silversmith, became the first Lord Mayor of Dublin in 1665. There was an interesting instance in 1685 of a goldsmith, acting as city treasurer, petitioning the council for some £1100 plus interest which he had loaned the city to enable it to pay off some pressing debts. This gives some indication of the wealth of the goldsmiths during the late seventeenth and early eighteenth centuries.

The duty that was introduced in England and Scotland in 1719 was not applied to Ireland until 1729: 'An Act for laying several duties upon coaches, berlins, chariots, calashes, chaises, and chairs, and upon cards and dice and upon wrought and manufactured gold and silver plate imported or made in Ireland'. The duty became payable from 25 March 1730. The figure of hibernia was added to the crowned harp. Date letter and maker's mark showed that the duty had been paid. It was not until 1752 that it became illegal to sell plate without this mark.

From 1777, seven years before it was introduced in England there was provision for an 'export rebate' of the duty paid on any silver or gold sold outside Ireland. This came to an end in 1786 with the introduction of the licencing system in lieu of duty that had already been tried in England prior to the restoration of duty in 1784. Licencing was abandoned three years later and the 6d duty re-imposed.

In 1784 a new assay office was opened at New Geneva, near Waterford, to deal with the trade brought by continental jewellers and watchmakers who had left the mainland of Europe because of religious or political views. It was declared that the marks of this office should be different from those in use in Dublin. The venture, however, was very short lived. The office was closed down within three months of its establishment and it is unlikely that silver was ever marked there. As from 1792 the goldsmiths had to pay both for their licence and the 6d duty. The Act of Union in 1801, like the Act of 1707 for Scotland, while leaving the laws relating to hallmarking as they were, made provision for them to be changed by the joint Parliament if and when they deemed it necessary. This was the case with the Plate Assay (Ireland) Act of 1807 which brought the conducting of the Dublin Assay Office in line with its English counterparts. Duty which applied in England and Scotland was therefore extended to the Dublin goldsmiths (this was not as bad as it sounds because since 1805 they had been paying duty at the rate of 1s (5p) an ounce). Thus, once the king's head was added, the figure of hibernia was confirmed as a supplementary mark to the harp in identifying a piece to be of Dublin manufacture and of sterling standard. The hibernia had completely lost its relevance as a duty mark.

The Government of Ireland Act 1920, declared all plate assayed in the Republic of Ireland after 1923 foreign for the English customs. So, although most of the plate marked in Dublin can be labelled British, that made after 1923 must be considered Eirean.

There were a number of unofficial provincial centres in Ireland which made plate in small quantities. The only town responsible for a large output was Cork. The others were Limerick, Youghal, Galway, Kinsale, Londonderry and Kilkenny.

THE MAKERS

Makers, the marks they used and their history can be one of the most exciting and rewarding parts of the study of silver. Knowledge of the background of the man who was responsible for the production of a piece can bring that piece to life. All pieces of silver pose the same questions. Is it a good design? Is the workmanship of good quality? Was the piece made actually by the man whose mark it carries or by a journeyman in his workshop? Did the maker specialise in this particular aspect of the trade or was he a general smith? What class of patron was he working for – other retailing smiths, the nobility, aristocracy, wealthy untitled or the new middle class?

These questions, so easily posed are not always so easy to answer. In the case of the fashionable smiths the history and development of their individual art and prosperity, or lack of it, can be traced through their own work.

Makers' marks have changed considerably in character since the thirteenth century, although the scope for change would not seem to be very great. The early makers' marks very often do not incorporate an initial at all, but the device, or identifying sign under which a smith worked. These signs, which were common to all trades until the end of the eighteenth century usually carried no writing and were designed to convey the identity of the craftsman and his craft to a largely illiterate public. The sign would very often be a rebus on the name of the smith. A good example is William Mutton, one of Chester's most prolific Elizabethan silversmiths whose sign was a sheep's head, as was his mark; a London goldsmith of the fifteenth century, John Clef uses a key as a rebus. Some of the marks, even as early as the fifteenth century are only the makers' initials or initial, although this is very uncommon before 1530 (possibly the influence of the increase in literacy following the invention of the printing press and its adoption for producing books in 1470). Throughout the sixteenth century the marks evolved the symbol only. Marks gradually gave way to marks incorporating both the makers' initials and his sign. One example of this is a London smith of the initials HC whose sign, incorporated into his punch is a hand grasping a goldsmith's planishing hammer. By 1630 it was exceptional to find a sign-only marked piece. The normal mark was the maker's initials, either with or without his sign.

The 1697 Act which raised the standard of the silver to be used to 95.84 per cent of pure silver (a decrease in the permissable amount of alloy used from 750 parts per 1000 to 416 parts per 1000 – a decrease of some 55 per cent!) also prohibited the old maker's marks, legislating that each goldsmith should have a new type of mark, 'the workers mark to be expressed by the first two letters of his surname'. The first reason for the changing of the maker's mark is obvious – to differentiate the work made under the new standard completely from that made and assayed under the old. There is, however, another possible reason which would explain the lack of objection to the unreasonable and expensive demand of the new Act. There had been a bad fire at the assay office in November 1681. It is likely that the meticulously kept records of makers' names and marks which had been kept up, probably at least from the introduction of the 1478 series of date letters, were destroyed. The loss of these lists, pieces of paper (always used by the Goldsmiths' Company to keep their records in preference to parchment which can quickly become worn) attached to a strip of solid lead, the makers' names appearing in a column on the paper opposite their marks, would have been a serious blow to the company. Under these circumstances they would have been delighted at the change of style of the mark because it meant that every working goldsmith would have to re-register. There is further evidence that the ancient records were lost in the 1681 fire because the only positive record of makers' marks before 1697 is a copper plate struck just with the makers' mark punches of makers whose work is found in the period 1675 to 1697. This was possibly an attempt to replace the lost records after 1681 which was either abandoned, or has become detached in time from the papers. The copper plate is of little use in itself as it is merely a repetition of makers' marks that are frequently found on London pre-1697 plate. What it does provide however is an interesting idea of the average working life of the smiths of that period because some of the marks struck on the plate are identical or extremely similar to those registered after June 1720 when the old sterling standard was restored.

The new standard makers' marks which were introduced in 1697 as the result of the Act are a perfect example of what can happen if a person, without adequate knowledge of a trade or craft but is full of good ideas, is given rein to draft legislation. In the new record books, which open on 15 April 1697, a day short of three weeks after the introduction of the new Britannia marks there are no fewer than five makers whose surname begins with 'Lo' and whose marks incorporate these initials. In the case of the initials, 'Co', the degree of confusion is ridiculous. There are 19 different goldsmiths in this category alone. Another two were registered after 1720 – this must have caused great confusion at the assay office especially since a worn or badly

*A Quatrefail tankard (one
of two known, both by
the same maker) made in
1678 in London by A.R.*

struck 'go' makers mark punch can easily be read, 'Co'.

There is nothing to explain why the 1697 record books don't start until 20 days after the introduction of the new marks featuring Britannia and the lion's head erased. The delay has produced an amusing rarity – pieces struck with the old standard makers mark and the new accompanying punches. The last date letter of the old cycle, a small Gothic 't' is also found with both post 15 April makers' marks and Britannia accompanying marks – possibly because of a mix up in punches but more likely due to a shortage of the date letters for the new cycle as this combination is not uncommon.

The 1719 Act which re-introduced the sterling standard, while leaving Britannia as an alternative working material from 1 June 1720 also provided for the re-introduction of the 'old standard' maker's mark. Makers were expected to register and use each punch according to its standard. In order to avoid confusion, these two punches, when registered at Goldsmiths' Hall were often marked in the ledger with a small 'NS' for Britannia marks or 'OS' for sterling standard makers' marks. Trust in the goldsmiths to use the appropriate mark is well illustrated in that occasionally (I stress occasionally, not wanting to libel the Goldsmiths Company) pieces are to be found which are marked with a Britannia type standard maker's mark and Britannia standard accompanying marks, but with or without sign of any assay scrape taken which are of sterling standard. Another occurence is a new standard maker's mark accompanying sterling marks which overstrike the marks of the higher standard. The trap so cunningly set by the goldsmith was narrowly avoided by the servants of the assay office.

The Act of 1738, which was principally aimed at

reducing the amount of 'duty dodging' that had been taking place since 1720 had one other section that affected the makers and their marks. This simply made it unnecessary for a maker to have to register his Britannia punch and indeed every goldsmith in the country was required by the Act to have his previous punch destroyed or defaced and a new one made 'of a different character or alphabet'. This Act applied specifically to the provincial offices in addition to London and although it mentions assay offices at York, Bristol and Norwich, this is likely to be because the people responsible for the drafting of the Act did little research rather than the continued operation of these offices. The need for a different punch for Britannia standard had probably past by 1739. But ten years earlier and since 1720 many if not more silversmiths were still working the more expensive metal than had changed over to the 'old standard'. The change by the makers back to sterling appears to have been connected more with the 23-year habit of the older generation of goldsmiths who, having worked so long in the softer metal found it easier to stay with it than work in the harder cheaper alternative. Their customers seemed happier with the Britannia plate while the younger smiths, many of whom made some fine 'duty dodging' pieces, found that they were better able to compete with their seniors and among themselves, working in sterling silver.

After the petitioning of the leading makers of the towns of Birmingham and Sheffield, a committee of enquiry was appointed by the House of Commons. Part of the committee's report, known as the Parliamentary return of 1773 is an invaluable document. Not only does it list the number of ounces assayed at London and the three operating provincial offices but it puts forward the evidences of witnesses concerning frauds perpetrated by the manufacturers and vendors of silver and plate of London, Birmingham and Sheffield. It also gives a list of all the members of each company in 1773 together with the name of the assay master. Some parts are worth quoting:

Witness Francis Spilsbury, who made some fine silver said that 'he had been several times at Goldsmiths' Hall to treat the workmen with drink and thinks it of consequence to be on good terms with the scrapers as they have a power of showing favour in passing work, for when his plate has been objected to he has known those difficulties removed by giving liquor at the Hall. . . .'

Mr. James Davenport (a journeyman working for Ebenezer Coker) informed the Committee that 'about three years ago Mr. Coker received a pair of Sauce Boats from a gentleman in London for old silver . . . he broke the handle off and found it loaded with solder made of Brass and silver, the boats being marked at Goldsmiths' Hall . . . that the witness rather chooses to buy silver of a refiner than old silver. (It is here understood, I think that he refers to old silver *with* hallmarks) because from a refiner he knows what he buys.'

Mr. Albion Cox, a refiner in Little Britain said that 'he had much experience in buying old silver, and *never* bought a tankard of London make and marked with the Goldsmiths' Hallmark without first examining the handle as there had often been found pieces of brass, copper, and solder within the handle. . . .'

The agent to Hoyland & Co of Sheffield produced his own defence for the silversmiths of his town, because on hearing that the London Goldsmiths' Company intended to charge some of them, together with some Birmingham makers of fraud, he went out and bought a pair of bottle tickets, a buckle, a table spoon and various other small pieces including a pair of unmarked buttons, all of which with the exception of the buttons carried gold-smiths hall assay marks. Rather than submitting the full pieces for assay he carefully cut out particular pieces for easier identification, and labelled each of the pieces. The bottle tickets were 11 oz only to the troy pound pure (91.6 per cent) while the teaspoons were only 10 oz 16 dwt (88.75 per cent) the unmarked buttons had the distinction of being 7 oz $5\frac{1}{2}$ dwt (60.63 per cent). All the pieces were under the permitted standard of 11 oz 2 dwt. What the committee is not told, which I suspect may have been the case, is how much Mr. Holbrook invested on behalf of his masters in buying small pieces to have as many of substandard silver to illustrate his point about the unreliability of the London assay office.

A Mr. Floyer informed the committee much along the lines that Mr. Cox had earlier said that 'when tankards or cups with the mark of *London* workmen are offered to him for sale he suspected they might have too much solder in the handles and always looked upon it as necessary to break those parts'.

Mr. Cox's testimony is very revealing for later he mentions that 'he now sells silver to the silversmiths at Sheffield 2 dwt worse than standard, though when he went first to that place it was the custom of the house he is concerned with to make all their silver standard until he told them that they passed silver at the London Goldsmiths' Hall some $2\frac{1}{2}$ dwt worse (1.15 per cent below standard) and then they reduced theirs to the same worseness. . . .'

Mr. Joseph Clerk informed the committee that: '11 oz 2 dwt (92.5 or sterling standard) of fine silver and 18 dwt of alloy mixed together will not be reported standard by

A pair of cake baskets, 27 cm, made in 1747 in London by Edward Wakelin.

any assay master. That the London refiners sell silver to their customers that is 2 dwt worse which is allayed as the Act directs. . . . Being asked the reason why 11 oz 2 dwt fine silver when melted down will not turn out as 11 oz 2 dwt fine silver he replied that every time that silver is refined it loses 2 dwt in the pound (12 oz) of its substance, that perfectly pure silver will emerge from the fire as 11 oz 18 dwt, the next day if returned into the fire as 11 oz 16 dwt (and so on). . . .'

Mr. Floyer when asked the same question gave very much the same answer, except the tone suggests that he is more pleased with himself.

'That Mr. Floyer appreciates that the standard for plate is the same as for coin in this kingdom . . . before he sells sterling silver to workmen he sends assays to Goldsmiths' Hall and when it is reported from thence standard he puts (adds) to it 1 or 1½ dwt of copper but never more and if a piece of plate was made from that silver it would pass at Goldsmiths' Hall as standard and that he has never had any of his silver cut (found substandard) since he has been in the trade, which is about 30 years . . . and being asked whether 11 oz 2 dwt of his fine silver and 18 dwt of copper will make silver of legal standard he said that it will be reported 2 dwt worse, which is in fact the remedy.'

The London makers were perturbed at the success of Old Sheffield plate which had by that time just reached its pinnacle in many ways as subsequent to the Act. The only marks allowed were the makers' names which had to be registered at Sheffield. One of the main inducements to make Old Sheffield Plate in exact imitation of the current styles for silver was removed. The witnesses had plenty to say about the plated wares:

Mr. Abraham Portal said: 'It is a common thing for

the makers of wares plated with silver at Birmingham and Sheffield to stamp four marks thereon which in size and shape imitate those struck at Goldsmiths' Hall . . . The witness produced a can plated with silver which he bought of the agents of a Sheffield manufactory which resembled silver very much . . . and believed that the marks were not put on with any fraudulent intention . . . that in his own shop he has not known plated work from silver without a long examination . . . he had dealt in plated wares ever since it came into use and never objected to the makers putting four marks thereon which he presumed were the maker's name and did not apprehend that they were put on with fraudulent design, but probably to gratify their customers that it made the work look more like silver, that he never knew a Sheffield or Birmingham man attempt to sell such work for silver.'

Mr. Richard Morson said: 'He had dealt in plated work for four or five years and that about a year since he forbid the four marks being put on the plate he bought, as he thought it seemed illegal, and that he forbid the four marks being put on his plated wares *before* he heard of an application from Birmingham and Sheffield to obtain assay offices.'

In the course of preparing this report all the assay office records from 1697 were handed over to the committee, all but two were returned. One is of considerable importance. It is the book of *Large Workers,* makers who made items for every day use such as candlesticks, bowls, mugs, teapots etc. for the period September 1759 to 7 March 1773 (the report is dated the 25 March that year), a period during which a large amount of plate was produced in a wider variety of styles than ever before in the history of British silversmithing. Another volume which went missing at the same time is the small workers book for marks registered from May 1739, the date when all the makers had to make new punches to July 1758. It would be nice to think that these volumes managed to escape the fire at the House of Commons in 1834 (if indeed they were still there then, and were not residing in one of the committee member's libraries) and are lying wrongly catalogued in a corner somewhere waiting to be rediscovered.

As I have already explained briefly there is no reason why the silversmith whose mark appears on a piece of English plate should have ever been seen, yet alone touched by that piece of plate. A goldsmith in England, as well as Scotland had to serve a seven-year apprenticeship in order to learn his craft. (This is the official version, in fact it took only about five years to teach an apprentice, the remaining two years was cheap labour for the master!!) Once he had finished his apprenticeship he would probably become a journeyman, working in his masters workshop for a daily wage – most of the fine silver of the eighteenth and early nineteenth centuries was made by journeymen goldsmiths whose names, although known can never be tied up with their work. The young goldsmith would then try to set up on his own. This obviously required the sort of capital that was not readily obtainable. But, having achieved independence, membership of the Goldsmiths' Company with its many advantages and, with any luck, a good clientele, the goldsmith would start employing people to aid his craft – a turner, a polisher, perhaps even some journeymen. Thus the business would expand until he was probably only involved in getting orders and keeping the books. Collecting orders was closely tied up with ideas on design.

Other ways in which people could register a mark was

through a widow inheriting her husband's business without knowing the first thing about the silversmith craft. This was particularly common during the eighteenth century when some of the finest silversmithing family fortunes were saved by the former master's widow. This is well illustrated by the fate of the Courtauld family of silversmiths. The firm was founded on the skills of Augustine Courtauld who took his son Samuel as an apprentice. Samuel inherited the business on the death of his father in 1751 and ran it until his own death in 1765. His widow took over the management and for a short while Samuel's apprentice and son in law George Cowles until her son Samuel Jnr. was old enough to take part in the business. Although it was not common for a woman to take on an apprenticeship as a goldsmith there are several examples. One is Sarah Cooke, who was apprenticed for seven years in 1733. She chose to take her freedom in 1747.

Probably the best known of all English goldsmiths is Paul de Lamerie who was, as his name suggests, a French Huguenot immigrant. He served his apprenticeship under another immigrant, Pierre Platel and became free of this fine craftsman in 1712. The work of Paul de Lamerie is unmistakeably Huguenot in the massive use of weight, both of metal and decoration. His work is basically of the French taste of the period, but adapted to the slightly more austere feelings of London society. Lamerie was soon patronised by the leaders of fashion and the nobility (there are some particularly fine examples of his work in the collection of the Duke of Bedford at Woburn Abbey which are usually on public display). His work bore little relation to that of his contemporary goldsmiths in London. His reputation and obvious success meant that he only had to introduce some new facet of design to a piece for it to be widely copied. One of the best and most famous techniques used in his massive workshop was the manner of his casting. The subjects of this casting were usually of mythical creatures, often connected with the sea, felt by Lamerie to be the closest element to silver.

Lamerie himself was responsible for some of the work produced in his workshop, and probably most of the work before 1725. There seems little doubt that not only his technique but the general high standard of work are the qualities that have made his silver among the most sort after pieces from England. When he died in 1751, the business was disbursed. It is interesting to note that Lamerie, who was one of the goldsmiths responsible for complaining to the London Company of the considerable number of pieces that were being made outside the law to avoid duty, engaged frequently in 'duty-dodging' techniques, specialising in items that were made on commission. There is a fine ewer with his marks on view in the Victoria and Albert Museum. The marks have been let in between the foot and body, one of the most common places at an enormous saving to somebody (customer or goldsmith).

Although the beginning of the eighteenth century saw the full effect of the immigrant Huguenots influence on English fashion, there was a general reluctance on the part of the monarchy as well as the leading peers to patronise these foreigners. They chose English goldsmiths like Anthony Nealme and Benjamin Pyne whose work was of the first order, often attempting (successfully) to imitate popular immigrant designs.

Anthony Nealme, who must rank as one of the greatest silversmiths of his period was one of the main exponents of the plain sides and simple lines that were 200 years later to be referred to and sought after as 'Queen Anne' style, a title which in no ways does credit to the art of this versatile silversmith.

One Huguenot goldsmith whose design is worthy of mention is David Willaume. This goldsmith specialised in making vast pieces of plate for the houses of the nobility. He produced many fine two-handled cups, ewers and basing in the Huguenot vein. One fine example is a smaller than average ewer with the date letter for 1700/01 which is on display at the Victoria and Albert Museum.

During the eighteenth century the rôle of the goldsmith changed. Before 1770 there was still the freedom of form that had been introduced some 85 years earlier. This gave rise to such work as the few pieces made between 1742 and 1745 by Nicholas Sprimont whose ideas regarding the design were unique in his period. The work was decorated with all kinds of insects, shells, stones, leaves and other natural subjects. He is even known to have made salt cellars by simply using a large, suitably trimmed shell as the main cast and adding feet, cast from smaller versions of the same shell. Unfortunately, he left the craft in order to take an interest in what was to become the 'Chelsea' porcelain factory where it is not difficult to identify the same preoccupation with nature.

Apart from the few exceptional artist-craftsmen such as Nicholas Sprimont, the general trend during the middle years of the eighteenth century was toward specialisation. One firm specialised in providing cast handles and feet, while another workshop, like that of Richard Rugg, John Tute and Dorothy Mills, specialised in making salvers and waiters. Others specialised in the production of tea caddies, candlesticks, and boxes.

COURTESY OF SOTHEBY & CO

A set of four candlesticks
19 cm made in 1739 in
London by John Gould.

By 1761 there were 300 members of the Goldsmiths' Company and the craft was expanding at such a rate that it was unusual for a workshop to employ less than 10 people. Under this atmosphere of expansion there was a significant fall in the quality of much of the domestic plate. Customers often required size at the expense of solidity and it is now that the weight of an item comes to suggest the quality of workmanship involved. For the 60 years from 1770 to 1830 it is remarkable how similar in weight pieces in basically the same form but by different goldsmiths can be. A large difference indicates either that one of the pieces is exceptional or below average. An example of this (although very approximate) is cream jugs. A good one made about 1770 will weigh about 4 oz troy while it is possible to find jugs very similar in appearance that weigh as little as 2 oz. The makers whose wares can usually be relied upon for the quality of their craftsmenship are listed in the tables.

Probably the most famous English woman silversmith is Hester Bateman, a name which will mean something even to those who have no interest in silver. The Bateman family made a speciality of making small pieces, bottle tickets, sugar tongs and generally pieces which could with advantage be decorated with 'bright cutting' (a method of engraving by which a one-sided chisel is used, leaving a bright facet after each cut which was popular from about 1780 to 1805). The small pieces, especially the bottle tickets show a great deal of imagination in design. Their often completely original forms make them desirable collectors pieces. Unfortunately, the rest of the wares produced in the Bateman workshop are of indifferent standard, both in the weight of metal employed and the craftsmanship of manufacture. Probably this indicates the lack of supervision given to the journeymen. The situation that brought the Bateman family success in their own time was the sudden fashion for the neo-classical as the result of the writings of Robert Adam. Vase shapes and ovals are ideal for light-gauge silver. The eye is caught by the elegance of the design before being brought back to the stark reality of the lack of quality.

While there are literally hundreds of more reliable silversmiths working in London at this time, Hester Bateman, with her 40 years of female control at a time when the fashion for silver was becoming delicate has, gained a mysticism beyond any of her rivals.

The next development after the simple Adam designs of the seventies and eighties was an extreme desire to imitate the great classical civilisation. Work required to meet this sort of demand was of a very high calibre which resulted in the emergence of such fine silversmiths as Paul Storr and Benjamin Smith. Paul Storr had the advantage of having been apprenticed to one of the great neo-classical silversmiths, Andrew Fogelburg, who had come to England from Sweden before 1773 (the exact date is mislaid in the missing record book, but he is listed in the Parliamentary return of 1773). As soon as Storr received his freedom, Fogelburg appears to have retired. Paul Storr, who did not get on too well with partners throughout his career started as a master in partnership with William Frisbee. This was short lived because only seven months later Storr registered his solo maker's mark. In 1807 he was persuaded to take over the running of the workshops of Messrs. Rundell Bridge and Rundell in Dean Street, while his great contemporary, Benjamin Smith, was busy working for the same firm in Greenwich. Storr and Smith had the imagination and technical skill; Rundell's had the clientele. The situation worked well for Smith until 1814 when he left to work on his own commission before joining his son in partnership in 1816. In 1819 Storr left Rundell too and opened a large retail premises in Bond Street in 1822.

Later run by John Mortimer, the project was not as successful as anticipated. Storr's nephew I. S. Hunt, who was later to emerge as a leading silversmith himself joined the partnership. Storr retired in 1838. The size of Rundell Bridge and Rundell's workshop at Dean Street was exceptional. Over 100 people were employed. All worked plate that had been commissioned from Storr and left the workshop carrying his maker's mark. The produce of this workshop was exceptional. Few pieces of poor craftsmanship were produced with the exception of the flatware, spoons and forks which were generally, being one of the easiest jobs, left to juniors. The results of this policy remain with us.

One firm which really left its mark on the ordinary domestic wares of the 20 years between 1808 and 1822 was that of Rebecca Emes and Edward Barnard. The latter had been leading journeyman to John Emes, Rebecca's husband. The pattern for this partnership had already been set by John Emes. His work was always original and almost without exception of outstanding quality. The firm specialised in 'holloware', pieces of domestic silver, teasets, bowls, pap boats, bottle tickets. It sold wares to retailing silversmiths and its versatility was as great as the legendary Huguenot silversmiths of a hundred years before. It could produce two similar objects of violently different design in order to satisfy two different customers.

The goldsmiths of Chester have only one name which, regardless of the generation, sum up the peak of their craft in the eighteenth century. This is the name of

Richardson. Three generations of this remarkable family span some 87 years and monopolise the craft. In the nineteenth century there were no outstanding smiths, although some good spoons and forks are found with the mark of John Sutters of Liverpool.

Matthew Boulton, one of the most interesting entrepreneurs of the eighteenth century had a connection with Chester in that it was to this office that he and his partner James Fothergill had to send all their plate for assay before his efforts to open an assay office in Birmingham were successful. The respect that was held for two very different men by the same Goldsmiths' Company is most avidly illustrated by a report from Mr. Scasebrick, the Chester assay master, to the parliamentary enquiry in 1773: 'that the plate which has been sent by Messrs. Boulton & Fothergill of Soho near Birmingham to be assayed and marked at the Chester Assay Office has generally been 2 or 3 dwt *above* standard. . . . the witness never heard of Mr. Richardson's plate being objected to as under standard and believes it not in the power of any man living to object to it.' The death of Richard Richardson resulted in a temporary slump in the amount of plate being assayed in Chester, reaching a low of 161 ounces in the year 1769.

Birmingham's fortune was created by one man who, by his skill in trade and expertise in bringing pressure to bear on opponents brought employment to the population and established the basis for later growth in the assay office that was to handle so many thousands of small pieces of silver by the turn of the century. One of Boulton's apprentices, Edward Thomasson, became one of Birmingham's leading citizens in the first quarter of the nineteenth century. He was appointed as a diplomat receiving honours from many European countries before returning to his home city to run his business. The wares from this were at least equal to those of any other provincial smiths. The other Birmingham makers tended to specialise in small pieces – buttons, boxes, purses, seals, buckles etc.

The outstanding Exeter maker is John Elston who was responsible, from the outset of the 1701 Act, for establishing Exeter as an assay town for the production of a few very fine pieces. His rival was John Mortimer who although more prolific is not recorded as making pieces of the same size as Elston.

In Sheffield the manufacturers all produced the same sort of goods at the same sort of price. Thomas Law, one of the agitators for the appointment of an assay office, stands out as the most enterprising. He produced not only knives as he had before 1773, but a whole range of domestic silver of very acceptable quality.

The goldsmiths of Newcastle were unique among the provincial towns in that from about 1730 they tended to specialise in mugs. These were sold all over Britain. The leading makers were John Langlands and John Robertson – skilled silversmiths who had the foresight to have their makers' punch registered at London to overcome London bias against provincial makers. On John Langlands death the business was taken over by his widow, Dorothy. Langlands had been the driving force behind a very successful provincial company. His death marked the end of Newcastle's era of goldsmithing prosperity.

York is the only major town without one credit in the Report of 1773, a fact that is difficult to explain due to the re-opening of the assay office in 1776. The whole assay office appears to have revolved around one partnership, with the local small makers making occasional contributions. The partnership of John Hampston and John

Prince lasted in one form or another of its evolution until 1858 when, because of insufficient use, the office was closed.

The study of provincial makers and their marks is interesting, not only because they were never a great number but because of the rôle they and their company played in the local community. The field is very large and to a great extent uncovered. This adds the additional incentive of finding original material relating to the goldsmiths, their trade, workshops, misdeeds or achievements. The information is there, waiting to be found and correlated. The present state of knowledge brings the goldsmiths one step nearer to life.

TABLES OF MAKER'S MARKS

DUBLIN

1700–1730
WA	William Archdall
EB	Edward Barrett
RC	Robert Calderwood
IC	John Cuthbert
IH	John Hamilton
MH	Michael Hewitson
DK	David King
HM	Henry Matthews
TP	Thomas Parker
TS	Thomas Slade
CT	Christopher Thompson
TW	Thomas Walker

1730–1770
AB	Alexander Brown
IC	John Christie
WC	William Currie
JD	James Douglas
EF	Esther Forbes
DK	David King
TK	Thomas Kinslea
AL	Antony Lefebure
IL	John Laughlin
BM	Bartholomew Mosse
IP	John Pittar
AR	Alexander Richards
RW	Richard Williams
SW	Samuel Walker
WW	William Williamson

1770–1820
ILB	John Le Bas

IB	John Buckton
WC	William Cummins
IE	James England
DE	Daniel Egan
IF	John Fry
II	Joseph Jackson
TJ	Thomas Jones
TK	Thomas Kinslea
SN	Samuel Neville
WN	William Nowlan
J.P	John Pittar
JP	John Power
WR	William Rose
RS	Richard Sawyer
IS	James Scott
GW	George Wheatley
MW	Matthew West
RW	Robert William

1820–1850
GA	George Alcock
IB	John Buckton
ILB	John Le Bass
EC	E. Crofton
EJ	Edmund Johnson
WL	William Lawson
CM	Charles Marsh
PM	Patrick Moore
MN	Michael Nowlan
EP	Edward Pome
JS	James Smythe
TWY +	Edward Twycross
PW	Peter Walsh

GLASGOW

1819–1850
PA	Peter Arthur
A & T	Aird & Thompson
JC	James Crichton
RG & S	Robert Gray & Sons
JL	John Law

DMcD	David McDonald
AM	Alexander Mitchell
JM	John Mitchell
LFN	Luke Newlands
WP	William Parkins
DCR	Duncan Rait

EDINBURGH

1700–1759

WA	William Aytoun	IG	John Gilsland
HB	Henry Beathune	G & K	Gilsland & Ker
CD	Charles Dixon	AH	Alexander Henderson
AE	Alexander Edmonstone	FH	Francis Howden
HG	Hugh Gordon	PM	Peter Mathie
RG	Robert Gordon	DM	David Marshall
WG	William Ged or Gilchrist	PR	Patrick Robertson
RI	Robert Inglis	WR	William Robertson
AK	Alexander Kincaid	AS	Alexander Spence
IK	James Ker	WT	William and Jonathan
MK	Colin McKenzie	IT	Taylor
RK	Robert Ker	IW	John Walsh
K & D	Ker & Dempster	AZ	Alexander Zeigler
EL	Edward Lothian	IZ	John Zeigler
EO	Edward Oliphant		
LO	Lawrence Oliphant	**1800–1850**	
IR	James Rollo	MC	Matthew Craw
GS	George Scott	E & Co	Elder & Co
WS	Walter Scott	GF	George Fenwick
MY	Mungo Yorstoun	RG & S	Robert Gray & Son
		AH	Alexander Henderson
1760–1800		GMH	George McHattie
RB	Robert Bowman	JMc	John McKay
GC	George Christie	JM	Jonathan Millidge
RC	Robert Clark	J & WM	James and William
W & PC	William and Peter Cunningham		Marshall
WPC	William and Peter Cunningham	M & C	McKay & Chisholm
		M & F	McKay & Fenwick
ID	James Dempster	M & S	Marshall & Sons
JD	James Douglas	JN	James Nasmyth
AE	Alexander Edmonstone	PS	Peter Sutherland
AG	Alexander Gairdner	LU	Leonard Urquhart

SHEFFIELD

1773–1820

GA & Co	George Ashforth & Co	WD	William Damant
MF	Fenton, Creswick & Co	GE & Co	George Eadon & Co
RC		RG	R. Gainsford
		IG & Co	John Green & Co

IH & Co	J. Hoyland & Co	JB	James Burbury
IL	John Law	TJ & NC	T.J. and N. Creswick
TL	Thomas Law	JC	J. & N. Creswick
RM	Richard Morton & Co	NC	J. & N. Creswick
RM & Co	Richard Morton & Co	D & S	Dixon & Sons
IP & Co	John Parsons & Co	AH	Aaron Hadfield
IR & Co	John Roberts & Co	MH & Co	Martin Hall & Co
SR GC & Co	Samuel Roberts & Co	H & H	Howard & Hawksworth
GC	George Cadman	HE & Co	Hawksworth, Eyne & Co
NS & Co	Nathaniel Smith & Co	WK & Co	Walter Knowles & Co
HT	Henry Tudor	RM	Remy Martin and Edward
TL	Thomas Leader	EH	Hall (Martin Hall & Co)
IW & Co	John Winter & Co	S & N	Stafford & Newton
ITY & Co	John T. Younge & Co	T & IS	T & I Settle
		W & H	Walker & Hall
SCY & Co	S.C. Younge & Co	HW & Co	Henry Wilkinson & Co

1820–1870
HA	Henry Archer & Co

NEWCASTLE

1702–1720
Ba	Francis Batty
Bi	Eli Bilton
Bu	John Buckle (of York)
Ki	James Kirkup
La	John Langwith
Ra	John Ramsay
Yo	John Younghusband

1720–1790
FB	Francis Batty
GB	George Bulman
WB	William Beilby
DC	David Crawford
IC	Isaac Cookson
WD	William Dalton
JG	John Goodriche
IK	James Kirkup
JL	John Langlands

IL	John Langlands and
IR	John Robertson
IM	John Mitchison
RM	Robert Makepeace
TP	Thomas Partis
RP RS	Pinkney & Scott
CR	Christian Reid
IS	John Stoddart

1790–1830
MA	Mary Ashworth
DD	David Darling
AK	Alexander Kelty
DL	Dorothy Langlands
IL	John Langlands
AR	Anne Robertson
CR	Christian and David
DR	Reid

103

IR	John Robertson	WL ⎤	
R & D	Robertson & Darling	CL ⎬	Lister & Sons
RS	Robert Scott	WL ⎦	
IW	John Walton	L & S	Lister & Sons
TW	Thomas Watson	CJR	Christian Reid (Jr)
		DR	David Reid
1830–1883		TS	Thomas Sewill
WL	William Lister	IW	John Walton
		TW	Thomas Watson

YORK

1700–1717		WW	Whitwell – 1821
Bu	William Busfield	JB	James Barber & Co
La	John Langwith	& Co	1825
Ma	Thomas Mangy	BC	James Barber, George
		& N	Cattle, William North
1776–1858			1828
IH	John Hampston and John	JB	James Barber, George
IP	Prince – 1798	GC	Cattle, William North
HP	John Hampston, John	WN	1834
& C	Prince, Robert Cattle –	B & N	James Barber, William
	1802		North – 1846 only
P	John Prince, Robert	JB	James Barber, William
& Co	Cattle – 1808	WN	North – 1856
RC	Robert Cattle, James	JB	James Barber – 1856
JB	Barber – 1812	also :–	
JB	James Barber, William	E.J	Edward Jackson c. 1810–25

CHESTER

1700–1720		RR	Richard Richardson
Ma	Thomas Maddock	WR	William Richardson
Ri	Richard Richardson		
Bu	Nathanial Bullen	1771–1830	
Ro	Thomas Robinson	JA	John Adamson
Du	Bartholomew Duke	IB	James Barton
Bi	Charles Bird	B & F	Matthew Boulton and
Pe	Peter Pemberton		James Fothergill
		JC	James Conway
1720–1770		NC	Nicolas Cunliffe
TM	Thomas Maddock	RG	Robert Green
BP	Benjamin Pemberton	IG	John Gilbert
RP	Richard Pike	WH	William Hull

RI	Robert Jones	JC	John Coakley
GL	George Lowe	IL	
EM	Edward Maddock	TL	John and Thomas Lowe
WP	William Pugh	JL	John Lowe
RR	Richard Richardson	PL	P. Leonard
GW	George Walker	RL	Robert Lowe
IW	Joseph Walley	JP	John Parsonage
		GR	George Roberts
		IR	John Richards
1830–1870		JS	John Sutters
FB	Francis Butt	GW	George Ward

BIRMINGHAM

1773–1820		FC	Francis Clark
MB	Matthew Boulton	WF	William Fowke
MB IF	Matthew Boulton and John Fothergill	H & T	Hilliard & Thomasson
		L & Co	John Lawrence & Co
C & B	Cocks & Bettridge	NM	Nathanial Mills
ML	Matthew Linwood	P & T	William Postan and George Tye
SP	Samuel Pemberton		
WP	William Pugh	ES	Edward Smith
IS	John Shaw	T & P	Joseph Taylor and John Perry
ET	Edward Thomasson		
IT	Joseph Taylor	REA	Robinson, Edkins & Aston
JW	Joseph Willmore	GU	George Unite
TW	Thomas Willmore	Y & W	Yapp & Woodward

1821–1850	
IB	John Bettridge

LONDON

1697–1720		PL	Pierre Platel
AS	Thomas Ash	Py	Benjamin Pyne
BU	Thomas Burridge	Sc	William Scarlett
CO	Augustine Courtauld (fleur de lis above)	SL	Gabriel Sleath
		Sp	Thomas Spackman
FO	Thomas Folkingham	WI	David Willaume
HA	Pierre Harache (crown above)		
LA	Paul de Lamerie (crown and star above)	1720–1770	
		La	Paul De Lamerie (crown above star above initials, fleur de lis below)
LO	Nathanial Lock		
ME	Louis Mettayer		
NE	Antony Nealme	SA	Stephen Adams

105

S W I A	Stephen Adams and William Jury
HB	Hester Bateman
IC	John Cafe
WC	William Cafe
T W C C	Thomas and William Chawner
BC	Benjamin Cooper
EC	Ebenezer Coker
FC	Francis Crump
DPW	Dobson, Prior & Williams
WF	William Fearn
IG	John Gould
EF	Edward Feline
WG	William Grundy
TH	Thomas Heming
DH	David Hennell
R D H H	Robert and David Hennell
IH	John Hyatt
PL	Paul De Lamerie (crown above star above initials above fleur de lis)
SM	Samuel Meriton
DM	Dorothy Mills
LP	Lewis Pantin
MP	Mary Pantin
WP	William Peaston or William Plummer
RR	Richard Rugg
W W P S	William Shaw and William Priest
DS RS	Daniel Smith and Robert Sharp
GS	George Smith
S G S S	George and S. Smith
IS	John Swift
NS	Nicholas Sprimont
RS	Robert Swanson

ET	Elizabeth Tuite
JT	John Tuite
T & W	Turner & Williams

1771–1820

JA	Joseph Angell
HB	Hester Bateman
PB AB	Peter and Anne Bateman
PB IB	Peter and Jonathan Bateman (1790 only)
PB AB WB	Peter, Anne and William Bateman
WB	William Burwash
HC	Henry Chawner
HC IE	Henry Chawner and John Emes
IC	John Carter
RC	Richard Crossley
RC GS	Richard Crossley and George Smith
JE	John Emes
RE EB	Rebecca Emes and Edward Barnard
RE WE	Rebecca and William Emes
WE	William Eaton or William Eley
WE CE HE	William, Charles and Henry Eley
WE GP	William Eley and George Pierrepont
WE WF	William Eley and William Fearn
WE WF WC	William Eley, William Fearn and William Chawner
AF SG	Andrew Fogelberg and Stephen Gilbert
CF	Charles Fox or Crespin Fuller
WF	William Frisbee and
PS	Paul Storr

Mark	Maker
RG	Robert Garrard
SG	Samuel Godbehere
SG EW	Samuel Godbehere and Edward Wigan
SG EW	Samuel Godbehere Edward Wigan
IB	James Bult
WG	William Grundy
E W G F	William Grundy and Edward Fernell
TH IC	Thomas Hannam and John Crouch
JH	Jonathan Hayne
RH	Robert Hennell
RH DH	Robert Hennell and David Hennell
RH DH SH	Robert, David and Samuel Hennell
RH SH	Robert Hennell and Samuel Hennell
CK	Charles Kandler
JL	John Lias
IL HL	John and Henry Lias
RM RC	Robert Makepeace and Richard Carter
RM TM	Robert Makepeace and Thomas Makepeace
HN	Hannah Northcote
TN	Thomas Northcote
TO	Thomas Oliphant
LP	Lewis Pantin
TP ER	Thomas Phipps and Edward Robinson
TP ER JP	Thomas Phipps and Edward Robinson and James Phipps
TP IP	Thomas Phipps and James Phipps
WP	William Pitts
CR	Charles Rawlins
CR DR	Christian & David Reid

Mark	Maker
RR	Robert Rutland
TR	Thomas Robins
IS	John Scholfield
DS BS	Digby Scott and Benjamin Smith
DS RS	Daniel Smith and Robert Sharp
BS	Benjamin Smith
BS BS	Benjamin Smith & Son
GS	George Smith
GS WF	George Smith and William Fearn
MS	Mary Sumner
MS ES	Mary and Elizabeth Sumner
WS	William Sumner
WS RC	William Sumner and Richard Crossley
WT	Walter Tweedie
IW WT	John Walcelon and John Taylor
GW	George Wintle
TW JH	Thomas Wallis and Jonathan Hayne

1821–1850

Mark	Maker
GA	George Adams
JA	John Angel
JA JA	J. & J. Aldous
WB	William Bateman
MC	Mary Chawner
WE	William Eaton
WE CE HE	William, Charles and Henry Eley
CF	Charles Fox
RH	Robert Hennell
HH	Hyam Hyams
IL HL CL	John, Henry & Charles Lias
IL HL	John & Henry Lias

107

CR	Charles Rawlins and	ABS	Adey B. Savory
WS	William Summers	WRS	W. R. Smiley
CR	Charles Reilly and	PS	Paul Storr
GS	George Storer		

EXETER

1701–1720

AR	Peter Arno
El	John Elston
FR	Richard Freeman
Mo	John Mortimer
Ri	Edward Richards
Sy	Pentycost Symonds
TR	George Trowbridge
Wi	Richard Wilcocks

1720–1770

SB	Samuel Blachford
TB	Thomas Blake
IB	John Buck
DC	Daniel Coleman
IE	John Elston
WP	William Parry
TS	Thomas Sampson
RS	Richard Sams
JS	James Strong
IW	John Williams

1770–1830

| TE | Thomas Eustace |

GF	George Ferris (son of Richard)
RF	Richard Ferris
JH	Joseph Hicks
SL	Simon Lery
JO	John Osmont
IP	Isaac Parkin
WP	William Pearse
GT	George Turner
WW	William West (senior and junior)

1830–1882

JO	John Osmont
IP	Isaac Parkin
WP	William Pope
WRS	W. R. Sobey
SOBEY	W. R. Sobey
JS	John Stone
TS	Thomas Stone
JW	James Williams
JW & Co	James Whipple and Co.

Five of a set of twelve 'Trefid' topped spoons, made in London in 1698 by Joyce Issod.

TABLES OF DATE LETTERS

TABLE OF MARKS ON LONDON PLATE

Throughout the tables the date letters have been printed black on white (not white on black as in the shields) for ease of identification.

A	1678	1697	1716	1736	1756	1776	1796	1816	1836	1856
B	1679	1697	1717	1737	1757	1777	1797	1817	★37	1857
C	1680	1698	1718	1738	1758	1778	1798	1818	1838	1858
D	1681	1699	★19	★39	1759	1779	1799	1819	1839	1859
E	1682	1700	1720	1740	1760	1780	1800	1820	1840	1860
F	1683	1701	1721	1741	1761	1781	1801	★21	1841	1861
G	1684	1702	1722	1742	1762	1782	1802	1822	1842	1862
H	1685	1703	1723	1743	1763	1783	1803	1823	1843	1863
I	1686	1704	1724	1744	1764	★84	1804	1824	1844	1864
K	1687	1705	1725	1745	1765	1785	1805	1825	1845	1865
L	1688	1706	1726	1746	1766	★86	1806	1826	1846	1866
M	1689	1707	1727	1747	1767	1787	1807	1827	1847	1867
N	1690	1708	1728	1748	1768	1788	1808	1828	1848	1868
O	1691	1709	1729	1749	1769	1789	1809	1829	1849	1869
P	1692	1710	1730	1750	1770	1790	1810	1830	1850	1870
Q	1693	1711	1731	1751	1771	1791	1811	1831	1851	1871
R	1694	1712	1732	1752	1772	1792	1812	1832	1852	1872
S	1695	1713	1733	1753	1773	1793	1813	1833	1853	1873
T	1696	1714	1734	1754	1774	1794	1814	1834	1854	1874
U	———	1715	1735	1755	1775	1795	1815	1835	1855	1875

A	1876	1896	1916	1936	1956	1975
B	1877	1897	1917	1937	1957	1976
C	1878	1898	1918	1938	1958	1977
D	1879	1899	1919	1939	1959	
E	1880	1900	1920	1940	1960	
F	1881	1901	1921	1941	1961	
G	1882	1902	1922	1942	1962	
H	1883	1903	1923	1943	1963	
I	1884	1904	1924	1944	1964	
K	1885	1905	1925	1945	1965	
L	1886	1906	1926	1946	1966	
M	1887	1907	1927	1947	1967	
N	1888	1908	1928	1948	1968	
O	1889	1909	1929	1949	1969	
P	1890	1910	1930	1950	1970	
Q	1891	1911	1931	1951	1971	
R	1892	1912	1932	1952	1972	
S	1893	1913	1933	1953	1973	
T	1894	1914	1934	1954	1974	
U	1895	1915	1935	1955	——	

1719 Brittania Standard becomes voluntary and sterling marks are re-introduced.

1784–6 Octagonal intaglio King's Head duty mark used.

1786–1837 Oval King's Head duty mark used but in 1797 it can be found in silhouette.

1821 Leopard's Head becomes uncrowned.

1837–90 Queen's Head duty mark used.

1935 King and Queen's Head stamped to celebrate Silver Jubilee of George V.

111

A	1773	1798	1824	1849	1875	1900	1925	1950	1975
B	1774	1799	1825	1850	1876	1901	1926	1951	1976
C	1775	1880	1926	1851	1877	1902	1927	1952	1977
D	1766	1801	1827	1852	1878	1903	1928	1953	
E	1777	1802	1828	1853	1879	1904	1929	1954	
F	1778	1803	1829	1854	1880	1905	1930	1955	
G	1779	1804	1830	1855	1881	1906	1931	1956	
H	1780	1805	1831	1856	1882	1907	1932	1957	
I	1781	1806	1832	1857	1883	1908	——	——	
J	——	1807	——	1858	——	——	1933	1958	
K	1782	1808	1833	1859	1884	1909	1934	1959	
L	1783	1809	1834	1860	1885	1910	1935	1960	
M	★84	1810	1835	1861	1886	1911	1936	1961	
N	1785	1811	1836	1862	1887	1912	1937	1962	
O	★86	★12	1837	1863	1888	1913	1938	1963	
P	1787	1813	★38	1864	1899	1914	1939	1964	
Q	1788	1814	1839	1865	1890	1915	1940	1965	
R	1789	1815	1840	1866	1891	1916	1941	1966	
S	1790	1816	1841	1867	1892	1917	1942	1967	
T	1791	1817	1842	1868	1893	1918	1943	1968	
U	1792	1818	1843	1869	1894	1919	1944	1969	
V	1793	1819	1844	1870	1895	1920	1945	1970	
W	1794	1820	1845	1871	1896	1921	1946	1971	
X	1795	1821	1846	1872	1897	1922	1947	1972	
Y	1796	1822	1847	1873	1898	1923	1948	1973	
Z	1797†	1823	1848	1874	1899	1924	1949	1974	

1784–5   Octagonal intaglio King's Head duty mark used.

1785–97   Oval King's Head duty mark used.

1797   Double duty mark sometimes used.

1797–1833   Oval or silhouette King's Head duty mark used.

1833   William IV Head used in Oval.

1838   Queen Victoria's Head introduced until removal of duty in 1890.

1935   King and Queen's Head stamped to celebrate Silver Jubilee of George V.

TABLE OF MARKS ON CHESTER PLATE

A	1701	1726	1751	1776	1797	1818	1839	1864	1884	1901	1926	1951
B	1702	1727	1752	1777	1798	1819	1840	1865	1885	1902	1927	1952
C	1703	1728	1753	1778	1799	1820	1841	1866	1886	1903	1928	1953
D	1704	1729	1754	1779	1800	1821/2	1842	1867	1887	1904	1929	1954
E	1705	1730	1755	1780	★01	★23	1843	1868	1888	1905	1930	1955
F	1706	1731	1756	1781	1802	1824	1844	1869	1889	1906	1931	1956
G	1707	1732	G 57	1782	1803	1825	1845	1870	1890	1907	1932	1957
H	1708	1733	1758	1783	1804	1826	1846	1871	1891	1908	1933	1958
I	1709	1734	1759	★84	1805	1827	1847	1872	1892	1909	1934	——
J	——	——	——	——	——	——	——	——	——	——	——	1959
K	1710	1735	1760	1785	1806	1828	1848	1873	1893	1910	1935	1960
L	1711	1736	1761	★86	1807	1829	1849	1874	1894	1911	1936	1961
M	1712	1737	1762	1787	1808	1830	1850	1875	1895	1912	1937	1962
N	1713	1738	1763	1788	1809	1831	1851	1876	1896	1913	1938	
O	1714	1739	1764	1789	1810	1832	1852	1877	1897	1914	1939	
P	1715	1740	P 65	1790	1811	1833	1853	1878	1898	1915	1940	
Q	1716	1741	Q 66	1791	1812	1834	1854	1879	1899	1916	1941	
R	1717	1742	R 67	1792	1813	★35	1855	1880	1900	1917	1942	
S	1718	1743	1768	1793	1814	1836	1856	1881	——	1918	1943	
T	★19	1744	1769	1794	1815	1837	1857	1882	——	1919	1944	
U	1720	1745	U 70	1795	1816	1838	1858	1883	——	1920	1945	
V	1721	1746	V 71	1796	1817	——	1859	——	——	1921	1946	
W	1722	1747	W72	——	——	——	1860	——	——	1922	1947	
X	1723	1748	X 73	——	——	——	1861	——	——	1923	1948	
Y	1724	1749	Y 74	——	——	——	1862	——	——	1924	1949	
Z	1725	1750	(1775)	——	——	——	1863	——	——	1925	1950	

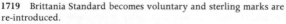

1719   Brittania Standard becomes voluntary and sterling marks are re-introduced.

1767–75   Date letter marks in serated punch.

1779   New town mark introduced.

1784–6   Octagonal intaglio King's Head duty mark used.

1786–1835   Normally silhouette King's Head duty mark used although it is sometimes found in an oval.

1835–40   Either silhouette or oval King's Head duty mark used.

1840–90   Oval Queen's Head duty mark used.

A	1701	1725	1749	1773	1797	1817	1837	1857	1877
B	1702	1726	1750	1774	1798	1818	1838	1858	1878
C	1703	1727	1751	1775	1799	1819	1839	1859	1879
D	1704	1728	1752	1776	1800	1820	1840	1860	1880
E	1705	1729	1753	1777	1801	1821	1841	1861	1881
F	1706	1730	1754	1778	1802	1822	1842	1862	1882
G	1707	1731	1755	1779	1803	1823	★43	1863	
H	1708	1732	1756	1780	1804	1824	1844	1864	
I	1709	1733	1757	1781/2	1805	1825	1845	1865	
K	1710	1734	1758	1783	1806	1826	1846	1866	
L	1711	1735	1759	★84	1807	1827	1847	1867	
M	1712	1736	1760	1785	1808	1828	1848	1868	
N	1713	1737	1761	★86	1809	1829	1849	1869	
O	1714	1738	1762	1787	1810	1830	1850	1870	
P	1715	1739	1763	1788	1811	1831	1851	1871	
Q	1716	1740	1764	q 89	1812	1832	1852	1872	
R	1717	1741	1765	r 90	1813	1833	1853	1873	
S	1718	1742	1766	f 91	1814	★34	1854	1874	
T	1719	1743	1767	t 92	1815	1835	1855	1875	
U	——	1744	1768	u 93	1816	1836	1856	1876	
V	1720				——	——	——	——	
W	★21	1745	1769	1794	——	——	——	——	
X	1722	1746	1770	1795	——	——	——	——	
Y	1723	1747	1771	1796	——	——	——	——	
Z	1724	1748	1772	——	——	——	——	——	

1721 Britannia Standard becomes voluntary and sterling marks are re-introduced.

1784–6 Octagonal intaglio King's Head duty mark used.

1886–97 Oval King's Head duty mark used.

1797–1816 Either oval or silhouette King's Head duty mark used.

1816–38 Oval King's Head duty mark used.

1833 William IV Head introduced.

1838–82 Oval Queen's Head duty mark used.

A	1721	1740	1759	1791	1815	1839	1864
B	1722	1741	1760/8	1792	1816	1840	1865
C	1723	1742	1769	1793	1817	★41	1866
D	1724	1743	1770	1794	1818	1842	1867
E	1725	1744	1771	1795	1819	1843	1868
F	1726	1745	1772	1796	1820	1844	1869
G	★27	1746	1773	★97	★21	1845	1870
H	1728	1747	1774	1798	1822	★46	1871
I	1729	1748	1775	1799	1823	1847	1872
J	——	——	——	——	——	1848	
K	1730	1749	1776	1800	1824	1849	1873
L	1731	1750	1777	1801	1825	1850	1874
M	1732	1751	1778	1802	1826	1851	1875
N	1733	1752	1779	1803	1827	1852	1876
O	1734	1753	1780	1804	1828	1853	1877
P	1735	1754	1781	1805	1829	1854	1878
Q	1736	1755	1782	1806	1830	1855	1879
R	1737	1756	1783	1807	1831	1856	1880
S	1738	★57	★84	1808	1832	1857	1881
T	1739	(1758)	1785	1809	1833	1858	1882
U	——	——	★86	1810	1834	1859	1883
W	——	——	1787	1811	1835	1860	
X	——	——	1788	1812	1836	1861	
Y	——	——	1789	1813	1837	1862	
Z	——	——	1790	1814	1838	1863	

1721–28 Sterling Standard mark sometimes faces to the right instead of the left.

*1733–90 Date letters are roman capitals and NOT italics.

1784–5 Octagonal intaglio King's Head duty mark used.

1786–96 Oval King's Head duty mark used.

1797–1820 Silhouette King's Head duty mark used.

1821–32 Oval King's Head duty mark used.

1832–42 Oval William IV King's Head duty mark used.

1840–84 Oval Queen's Head duty mark used.

A	1776	1787	1812	1837
B	1777	1788	1813	1838
C	1778	1789	1814	1839
D	1779	1790	1815	★40
E	1780	1791	1816	1841
F	1781	1792	1817	1842
G	1782	1793	1818	1843
H	1783	1794	1819	1844
I	——	1795	1820	1845
J	★84	1795	——	——
K	1785	1796	1821	1846
L	★86	1797	——	1847
M	——	1798	——	1848
N	——	1799	1824	1849
O	——	1800	1825	1850
P	——	1801	1826	1851
Q	——	1802	1827	1852
R	——	1803	1828	1853
S	——	1804	1829	1854
T	——	1805	1830	1855
U	——	1806	1831	——
V	——	1807	1832	1856
W	——	1808	1833	1857
X	——	1809	1834	1858
Y	——	1810	1835	
Z	——	1811	1836	

1784–5   Octagonal King's Head duty mark used.
1785–96   Oval King's Head duty mark used.
1796–1825   Silhouette King's Head duty mark used.
1825–39   Both oval and silhouette King's Head duty mark used.
From 1839   Queen's Head in oval.

TABLE OF MARKS ON SHEFFIELD PLATE

A	1779	1806	1824	1844	1868	1893	1918	1943	1968	1975
B	1783	1805	1825	1845	1869	1894	1919	1944	1969	1976
C	1780	1811	1826	1846	1870	1895	1920	1945	1970	1977
D	1781	1812	1827	1847	1871	1896	1921	1946	1971	
E	1773	1799	1828	1848	1872	1897	1922	1947	1972	
F	1774	1803	1829	1849	1873	1898	1923	1948	1973	
G	1782	1804	1830	1850	1874	1899	1924	1949	1974	
N	1777	1801	1831	1851	1875	1900	1925	1950		
I	★84	1818	——	1852	——	1901	1926	1951		
J	——	——	——	——	1876	——	——	——		
K	★86	1809	1832	1853	1877	1902	1927	1952		
L	1790	1810	1833	1854	1878	1903	1928	1953		
M	1789/94	1802	★34	1855	1879	1904	1929	1954		
N	1775	1800	——	1856	1880	1905	1930	1955		
O	1793	1815	——	1857	1881	1906	1931	1956		
P	1791	1808	1835	1858	1882	1907	1932	1957		
Q	1795	1820	1836	——	1883	1908	1933	1958		
R	1776	1813	1837	1859	1884	1909	1934	1959		
S	1778	1807	1838	1860	1885	1910	1935	1960		
T	1787	1816	1839	1861	1886	1911	1936	1961		
U	1792	1823	1840	1862	1887	1912	1937	1962		
V	1798	1819	1841	1863	1888	1913	1938	1963		
W	1788	1814	——	1864	1889	1914	1939	1964		
X	1797†	1817	1842	1865	1890	1915	1940	1965		
Y	1785	1821	——	1866	1891	1916	1941	1966		
Z	1796	1822	1843	1867	1892	1917	1942	1967		

From the opening in 1773 the town marks and date letter were amalgamated on small pieces of silver to prevent unnecessary damage.

1784–6   Octagonal intaglio King's Head duty mark used.

1786–96   Oval King's Head duty mark used.

1797   Double duty mark sometimes used.

1796–1824   Silhouette King's Head duty mark used.

1835   William IV Head introduced.

1824–40   Oval King's Head duty mark used.

117

A	1705	1730	1755	1780	1806	1832	1857	1882	1906	1931	1956	1975
B	1706	1731	1756	1781	1807	1833	1858	1883	1907	1932	1957	1976
C	★07	1732	1757	1782	1808	1834	1859	1884	1908	1933	1958	1977
D	1708	1733	1758	1783	1809	1835	1860	1885	1909	1934	1959	
E	1709	1734	★59	★84	1810	1836	1861	1886	1910	1935	1960	
F	1710	1735	1760	1785	1811	1837	1862	1887	1911	1936	1961	
G	1711	1736	1761	★86/7	1812	1838	1863	1888	1912	1937	1962	
H	1712	1737	1762	1788	1813	1839	1864	1889	1913	1938	1963	
I	1713	1738	1763	1789	1814	1840	1865	1890	1914	1939	1964	
J	—	—	—	1789	1815							
K	1714	1739	1764	1790	1816	★41	1866	1891	1915	1940	1965	
L	1715	★40	1765	1791	1817	1842	1867	1892	1916	1941	1966	
M	1716	1741	1766	1792	1818	1843	1868	1893	1917	1942	1967	
N	1717	★42	1767	1793	1819	1844	1869	1894	1918	1943	1968	
O	1718	1743	1768	1794	1820	1845	1870	1895	1919	1944	1969	
P	1719	★44	1769	1795	1821	1846	1871	1896	1920	1945	1970	
Q	1720	1745	1770	1796	1822	1847	1872	1897	1921	1946	1971	
R	1721	1746	1771	★97	★23	1848	1873	1898	1922	1947	1972	
S	1722	1747	1772	1798	★24	1849	1874	1899	1923	1948	1973	
T	1723	1748	1773	1799	1825	1850	1875	1900	1924	1949	1974	
U	1724	1749	1774	1800	1826	1851	1876	1901	1925	1950		
V	1725	1750	1775	1801	1827	1852	1877	1901	1926	1951		
W	1726	1751	—	1802	1828	1853	1878	1902	1927	1952		
X	1727	1752	1776	1803	1829	1854	1879	1903	1928	1953		
Y	1728	1753	1777	1804	1830	1855	1880	1904	1929	1954		
Z	1729	1754	1778	1805	1831	1856	1881	1905	1930	1955		

1779

1759   Thistle mark introduced.

1784–6   Octagonal intaglio King's Head duty mark used.

1786–96   Oval King's Head duty mark used.

1796–1823   Silhouette King's Head duty mark used.

1786–1826   Various forms of Castles used.

1823–40   Oval King's Head duty mark used.

1840–90   Oval Queen's Head duty mark used.

TABLE OF MARKS ON GLASGOW PLATE

A	1819	1845	1871	1897	1923	1949
B	1820	1846	1872	1898	1924	1950
C	1821	1847	1873	1899	1925	1951
D	1822	1848	1874	1900	1926	1952
E	1823	1849	1875	1901	1927	1953
F	1824	1850	1876	1902	1928	1954
G	1825	1851	1877	1903	1929	1955
H	1826	1852	1878	1904	1930	1956
I	1827	1853	1879	1905	1931	1957
J	1828	1854	1880	1906	1932	——
K	1829	1855	1881	1907	1933	——
L	1830	1856	1882	1908	1934	1958
M	1831	1857	1883	1909	1935	1959
N	1832	1858	1884	1910	1936	1960
O	1833	1859	1885	1911	1937	1961
P	1834	1860	1886	1912	1938	1962
Q	1835	1861	1887	1913	1939	1963
R	1836	1862	1888	★14	1940	
S	1837	1863	1889	1915	1941	
T	1838	1864	1890	1916	1942	
U	1839	1865	1891	1917	1943	
V	★40	1866	1892	1918	1944	
W	1841	1867	1893	1919	1945	
X	1842	1868	1894	1920	1946	
Y	1843	1869	1895	1921	1947	
Z	1844	1870	1896	1922	1948	

1841–90   Oval Queen's Head duty mark used.

119

TABLE OF MARKS ON DUBLIN PLATE

A	1720	1747	1773	1797	1821	1846	1871	1896	1916
B	1721	1748	1774	1798	1822	1847	1872	1897	1917
C	1722	1749	1775	1799	1823	1848	1873	1898	1918
D	1723	1750	D 76	1800	1824	1849	1874	1899	1919
E	1724	1751	E 77	1801	1825	1850	1875	1900	1920
F	1725	1752	E 78	1802	1826	1851	1876	1901	1921
G	1726	1753	G 79	1803	1827	1852	1877	1902	1922
H	1727	1754	H 80	1804	1828	1853	1878	1903	
I	1728	1757	I 81	1805	1829	———	1879	1904	
J	———	———	———	———	———	1854			
K	1729	1758	K 72	1806	1830	1855	1880	1905	
L	1730/1†	1759	L 83	1807	1831	1856	1881	1906	
M	1732	1760	M84	1808	1832	1857	1882	1907	
N	1733	1761	1785	★09	1833	1858	1883	1908	
O	1734	1762	1786	1810	1834	1859	1884	1909	
P	1735	1763	★87	1811	1835	1860	1885	1910	
Q	1736	1764	1788	1812	1836	1861	1886	1911	
R	1737	1765	1789	1813	1837	1862	1887	1912	
S	1738	1766	1790	1814	1838	1863	1888	1913	
T	1739	1767	1791	1815	1839	★64	1889	1914	
U	1740	1768	1792	1816	1840	1865	1890	1915	
V	———	———	———	———	1841	1866	1891	———	
W	1741/2	1769	1793	1817	1842	1867	1892	———	
X	1743/4	1770	★94	1818	1843	1868	1893	———	
Y	1745	1771	1795	1819	1844	1869	1894	———	
Y	1745	1771	1795	1819	1844	1869	1894	———	
Z	1746	1772	1796	1820	1845	1870	1895	———	

From **1730**   Figure of Hibernia used as duty mark.

For details of various Harps and Hibernias used between **1730** and **1772** refer to the booklet

Hall-marks On Dublin Silver published by the National Museum of Ireland.

1807–9   Rectangular King's Head duty mark used.

1809–21   King's Head duty mark in shield used.

1821–46   Many different shields used for all symbols, but these can be recognised by eliminating the other series first.

1838–90   Oval Queen's Head duty mark used.

READING HALLMARKS

British hallmarks don't lie. They have been developed over 700 years for the benefit of the bodies responsible for the welfare of the craft of goldsmithing. They promote the trade by reassuring the customer that he is getting what he pays for and provide these bodies with the information that is now of so much value to collectors. The information is basic – the name of the maker or makers, the place in which the piece was assayed, and the year in which it was assayed as an easy method of identifying the assay master. This is best shown by looking at the marks used in Edinburgh, where the assay masters initials were still used as a punch until 1759.

Reading hallmarks on silver is an acquired art, the more you do it, the easier it becomes. It is quite meaningless to sit down and try to learn the various date-letter cycles for each town without understanding the intricacies and differences between parallel series of date letters used in different towns.

Probably the easiest way to learn how to read hallmarks is to start with a known quantity. More plate has been assayed and marked in London than elsewhere in Britain. The chances of finding a London hallmark are much higher than finding one from another assay town.

All London marks used before 1780 are clear punches. They are usually large with symbols in high relief. They are found regularly in the same places on different items near the bowl of a spoon on the back of the stem (known as bottom marked) and on jugs or vessels with handles either just to the right of the handle or underneath. If there is no handle, marks are probably underneath but sometimes at the top on the side. Because the marks were in a vunerable position (e.g. on the underside of a cauldron-shaped salt cellar) they became worn and are now difficult to read. To make a mark easier to read, blow heavily on the piece over the mark. This will produce condensation on the cold metal and turn the surface matt for a few seconds. It will then be easier to read any small relief.

The first step in identification is to look for a town mark. If none is apparent, the first choice must be London. Next it is the turn of the variable date letter to be scrutinised. Is it a capital or small letter? What sort of script is the letter? What sort of shield is the letter in? Once these points are decided it is time to refer to the table. Is there a similar series? Do *all* the marks agree? If the mark in question has a king's head duty mark does the mark in the table look similar? Is the lion in the same shaped shield? If *all* things agree and only if, then an attribution can be made. Under no circumstances may a mark which does not tally with the tables be forced into an attribution. It should be checked again.

Marks made after 1780 London are usually found struck in an evenly spaced straight line. All marks except those of the maker were placed on a piece at once instead of one at a time as before. The exception to this is the octagonal intaglio kings head duty mark which was used with the re-introduction of duty in 1784. Marks made after 1782 on spoons and forks are found struck at the top of the back of the stem. The new bar system of punches weakened and distorted the stem – items such as cream jugs. The marks are now frequently found round the underside of the lip or around the outside of the foot. Teapots and pieces with flat bases are an exception to the straight-line rule. Many are marked on the bottom with the four main marks arranged around the maker's mark at the centre.

All the provincial assay towns used their town mark on pieces marked until 1773. This makes exact attribution much easier as neither the Exeter nor Newcastle assay offices survived to 1891 when the monarchs-head duty mark was dropped. But still the simple rules must be followed. However much the castle punch on a piece looks like an Edinburgh town mark, if the piece is also marked with a lion it must be English and in all probability Exeter. It becomes more difficult to read provincial hallmarks made after 1773, especially on smaller pieces. As in London, where teaspoons before 1782 were marked only with the lion sterling mark alongside the maker's mark, the makers tended to omit the town mark. (This may have been deliberate, since the customer preferred to think that the piece was London made.) The technique of reading the marks correctly on these pieces is a process of elimination. The odds are that the piece is London made and almost certainly after 1780. Here again it is important to remember that London marks will be in an evenly spaced straight line and the shield for the date letter will have a rounded base. In Exeter however, the shields used were absolutely rectangular and the king's head duty mark was struck separately. Alternatively, there is only a lion in an oval shield with a stippled background and the king's head and maker's mark (this lion, which is not shown in the tables was used from 1797 until 1808). The Chester equivalent has a badly formed lion with the corners of the shield cut, or later a very narrow shield. Georgian Chester is very scarce and unlikely to be found.

After 1821 both Exeter and London started marking even the smallest pieces with the town mark, even items like bottle tickets and collars for sauce bottles. In Newcastle from about 1790 the date letter was often left off in favour of the town mark. This was continued until about 1840. It can lead to confusion in putting an approximate date on a piece. One guide to dates is that before 1820 it is usual for pieces to have the duty mark to the *right* of the other marks. After 1820 the king's head is found to the left. It is uncommon to find a Birmingham made piece without its full accompanyment of hallmarks, but they are often not all struck in the same place. Vinaigrettes – small boxes fitted with a grille with a sponge soaked in smelling salts stored underneath were one of the more common pieces made in Georgian Birmingham. Examples are often marked with two assay marks on the lid. The other three are on the base (or vice-versa), indicating that the piece was regarded as a whole (the grille should be marked with an additional lion). Because of the many small pieces brought for assay in Sheffield, makers there used the clever device of a mark containing both the town mark and date letter. Sometimes the crown is upsidedown over the date letter. This differentiated the punch from earlier series.

York has not been mentioned so far. This town presents some very difficult problems which will occasionally even defeat people who have been handling silver for a long time. After the re-opening of the assay office in 1776 the marks used were similar to those in use in London. It was the exception rather than the rule for the town mark to be used. The best method of identifying silver assayed here is by the maker's marks, which are very distinctive (see list before the tables). The lion passant on small pieces marked between 1790 and 1810 is found facing to its right. Accompanying punches are often badly detailed, especially those of the leopard's head. Most mother of pearl fruit knives and forks have only a lion passant and duty mark. It is very unusual for these small pieces *not* to have been made and assayed in Sheffield.

It is important to remember that there is *only one* correct attribution regardless of how many alternatives there appear to be. This correct attribution can only be reached by practical reasoning and observation of simple rules. It is impossible for a piece with a king's head duty mark to have been made before 1784. A piece with a queen's head will have been made *after* 1837, the year of Queen Victoria's accession, and before 1891 when the duty was removed. Most Chester silver found was marked between 1890 and 1930. On Birmingham silver marked before 1784 the punches were struck separately, not in an evenly spaced straight line.

COLLECTING

Collecting silver sounds like an expensive hobby which, with the publicity that is given to the fluctuations in price, is not even that secure. Why be greedy? Antique silver is not something which can be learnt in a few weeks. It is a subject of such depth that the longer a person is acquainted with it, the more ignorant he realises he is. Who needs to collect rare coffee pots at thousands of pounds a piece when they can have a very fine collection of sugar tongs, none, of which cost more than £10.

The first question of any potential collector should be 'What shall I collect? The eventual choice should be governed by both budget and taste. Half the fun of collecting is adding new pieces to the collection. The subject of a collection should be capable of fulfilling this half. It is important from the point of view of interest to others that a collection is put together with care. Silver is an exceptionally intriguing and rewarding subject, but pieces collected at random seldom have the impact they could if they were related to other pieces (these other pieces need not necessarily be silver).

Once a possible choice has been made try and find out something about the history and development of the subject before buying anything. This is best done by visiting and talking to local antique dealers, examining any pieces they might have and enquiring the price they are asking for them. It is easy to learn from comparison why one example is better and more expensive than another. A visit to a local auction room which has sales of antiques will almost certainly reveal some pieces. The prices they fetch also act as a guide. The prices fetched at auction should be compared with the prices being asked in the shops. But remember that the dealer has to buy his stock somewhere and his only source of income is the difference between the buying and selling price.

A visit to the library will be helpful. Even if there is not a book written exclusively on the chosen subject the indices of the books in the collecting section will probably reveal much. There are only a very few subjects which have been given solo treatment but there will be chapters with relevant material.

When a background knowledge has been acquired it is safe to start a collection. It is important that to begin with, purchases are only made from reputable dealers. It is always worthwhile to pay just a little more for something that is obviously special, just as it is unnecessary to buy unwanted second-rate pieces because they are cheap – more often than not an apparently cheap buy is a bad buy. For satisfaction and investment it is always advisable to buy the quality pieces because it is these pieces that are the first to appreciate in a rising market and which hold their price best in a time of deflation.

It is unwise to buy a piece which has been mended. Repairs are usually quite apparent. As with the 'duty-dodgers' of the early eighteenth century a goldsmith has to use silver-solder for joints and mends. This solder, which has a lower melting point than silver is not such a bright colour, even when polished. When a piece is tested by blowing on it the solder shows up as a brownish tinge or line.

There are weak points which are liable to need mending on nearly every piece of wrought silver. With cream jugs the join of the handle to the body often becomes torn. The legs get pushed through and the foot gets creased. The spouts or lids of teapots are particularly vulnerable. There may be bruising around the feet where they have been dropped. The feet on salvers get broken or knocked off; the handles of beer mugs become damaged or tear away; salt cellars often have rubbed marks which detract heavily from their value; spoons become torn at the top of the bowl, forks with worn prongs have them levelled off; sugar tongs crack at the top of the bow, mustard pots get new lids; and muffineers split around the middle or acquire new tops which have different marks to their bases. These are just a few of the hazards which must be looked out for. They are all very common and can be found without too much difficulty.

One of the greatest pitfalls facing the collector is the fashion in the middle of the nineteenth century for highly decorative silver. This fashion led, many owners of Georgian silver (in the same way as their ancestors had melted old plate in exchange for new) to have this silver embellished with bunches of flowers. This 'improving' was done by placing a steel model on the inside of a piece, heating the silver and then hammering the silver onto the steel and working the design through. Pieces mutilated like this are *ruined* for a collection since it cuts the value of a piece by well over 50 per cent.

It is better to buy a piece without engraved initials or crests, as these are often later additions and have a detrimental effect on the value. Some pieces, like salvers, can look much better with an engraved coat of arms, a feature which in recent years has led to the engraving of many plain pieces with 'original' armorials. These pieces are ruined for collectors. The detection of the recently engraved pieces is often said to be a matter for experts although the practised eye can tell the difference without too much difficulty.

The decision on what sort of collection to make is a personal one. Each piece means much to the owner who knows the circumstance of each acquisition. Much fun can be had collecting the work of just one goldsmith because as every piece is added to the collection the owner gets a better insight into the mind of the workman – his peak years, his favourite patterns, and what, if anything was his speciality. There are two early nineteenth century London partnerships which would merit this approach. These are the work of Rebecca Emes and Edward Barnard and Thomas Phipps and Edward Robinson. Collecting by maker can also be applied successfully to Birmingham makers. The variety of wares produced, especially by such makers as Samuel Pemberton, Joseph Willmore and Joseph Taylor was remarkably diverse.

Another angle is to collect just the wares of one of the provincial assay offices. This form of collecting which is becoming increasingly popular will also prove interesting as the whims of the individual makers and the state of their craft at different times will emerge alongside local specialists. Makers' marks will be found which are not in the standard reference books. This creates the possibility of making a discovery from research in the registers, newspapers or local library of the chosen town.

Collecting by date letter is another possibility. Either collecting pieces manufactured in a specific year to make a comparison of the different styles and techniques used by the different makers in that year, or collecting by years and trying to have a similar piece to represent each year in a series. In this way the development of an item can be traced while at the same time the better makers can be identified. (The author knows of a collection of some 800 cream jugs, at least one for every year from 1720 to 1820. The only duplicates are of a different style to any others in a given year – the collection gives a unique insight into the evolution of cream jugs as well as illustrating the arrival and departure of the various fashions).

The collection of a single item is something that has to be entered into with great care. It is easy to become lost in the desire to acquire but there is not sufficient variety of some items to make their exclusive collection very meaningful.

These are just a few suggestions as to how to form a collection of some interest and aesthetic importance – not only to the owner, but to those with whom he chooses to share it with. The object of this chapter is to warn of the traps awaiting the inexperienced, while at the same time offering some basic advice which not only considers the pocket of the prospective purchaser, but also his subconscious, or not so subconscious need to feel that his collection is a good and worthwhile investment. Anybody who wants to collect silver, but is in any doubt about any aspect should consult one of the many good specialist dealers.

FAKES AND FORGERIES

The motive behind most fakes before about 1850 was usually political and personal. False marks were applied to a piece either because the smith, or smiths had been expelled from the guild of their towns and wanted their wares to seem as good as their competitors or because the work was of sub-standard silver and would thus have been destroyed rather than regularly marked.

Fake marks are scarce before the eighteenth century when one type makes its first appearance. This is a copy of the regular British hallmarks – both those of the London assay office and the provincial centres. The marks are put on the goods manufactured by expatriate British goldsmiths working in the colonies in order to satisfy his patrons – most of whom were used to looking for hallmarks on pieces they bought – that his wares were of an equally high standard as the genuinely hallmarked wares. These marks, which can be easily spotted because of their crudeness, usually date from the middle of the eighteenth century. Because these colonial marks imitate genuine hallmarks it is, until 1975 illegal for them to be sold in Britain.

The introduction of the 6d duty in 1719, as already mentioned, encouraged goldsmiths to transpose marks from pieces brought in for them to melt onto the newly made pieces to avoid payment of the duty. These pieces are still technically fake. Although they were genuine to the period when they were made they contravened the hallmarking laws. But, like the colonial pieces, the 1973 Hallmarking Act which came into force on 1 January 1975 made them legal for the first time. It is not these legitimate fakes that the collector should be wary of. These add interest to any collection, especially the colonial pieces which are probably far less common than their British equivalents.

It is remarkable that is was not until 1853 that an incredulous public was informed that there was nothing haphazard or modern about the date letters on silver plate and that these letters went back in regular cycles to the fifteenth century. This information, added to the already fast developing fashion for collecting 'old wares', led to a booming silver market. For the first time the general value of antique plate became inflated beyond its scrap price. The new collectors, however, were ill-informed. They trusted completely in the recently discovered date letters, a situation which led to a great amount of faking. The most amusing examples of fakes from this period are such things as 'Elizabethan' coffee pots which are to be found with marks for more than a hundred years before coffee was drunk in England. These have usually been made by reversing damaged chalices and communion cups.

Another method of producing absurdities was the transposing (in the manner of the duty dodgers) the marks of an early piece onto a supposedly 'antique' piece. These pieces are easily distinguished from duty dodgers because they are blatantly not the product of an eighteenth century silversmith. Most common are huge castors which are so much larger than anything actually produced at the time of their marks. Pieces of this type are of little more than interest value. No reputable dealer will sell them.

There are relatively few fake or forged silver hall-marks. Even the instances of false marks for modern fraud are usually easily distinguished by their soapy outline. It is remarkable how, after a little practice of handling genuine pieces of plate, a piece will suddenly feel 'wrong'. This is obviously something that only comes with experience, but it is good rule not to buy if in doubt.

The modern fashion of small pieces such as straining spoons, marrow scoops, tea caddy spoons and bottle tickets has produced many fraudulent examples. The stem of a teaspoon can be drawn a little and its bowl pierced. The bowl and stem of a tablespoon make a good marrow spoon; teaspoons with the middle of the stem removed make caddy spoons and what is easier than to take a cast from a bottle ticket? Beware!

A set of three ginger jars unmarked but made c. 1675 probably in London.

SOURCES OF REFERENCE

How to identify the use of a piece, and where to accurately determine its origin, maker, and value is a question often asked either by possessors or potential silver sellers. The answer is difficult and frequently unsatisfactory. The greatest problem is that the owner is interested in learning both the correct identification *and* the value of their piece. *It is only very rarely that these two questions can be answered simultaneously.*

Before trying to identify and value a piece it is necessary to overcome any mistrust of institutions. Museums exist to disperse knowledge, not only by displaying material of interest but in answering queries. There is at least one museum in every large town in Britain and their staff are completely trustworthy. They are always interested to see pieces in local possession and although not officially permitted to give their opinion as to value will certainly go out of their way to determine as much as possible about any piece they are shown. If they cannot give an on-the-spot answer they will ask to be left with the piece to do some further research or will suggest where the owner will be able to find out more.

It is unfair to ask an antique dealer to give a free valuation for two reasons. The difference between valuation for insurance and valuation for sale is usually in the region of 100 per cent, and it is part of a dealer's livelihood to charge for the service of using his professional knowledge and experience to make a correct valuation. A good dealer will always be prepared to offer his opinion of a price as long as he isn't asked for a free valuation at the same time.

From the collector's point of view there is one book which he must acquire at the opportunity, *English Goldsmiths and their Marks*, written by Sir Charles Jackson. This covers all the marks used in Britain since early times. While inaccurate in some places it is still the 'handbook' of the silver trade.

There are a series of books published in the form of price guides – silver catalogues which give an idea of price relativity although they are only expressing an opinion. They are, however, important books to own.

The London auction rooms can provide help in two ways. They will give a rough summary of any piece taken into them and guess what it might fetch while providing the best source of knowledge because they have regular sales with detailed catalogues. This makes it possible for the student to handle and watch large quantities of silver being sold every week.

With increased interest in antique silver over the last 10 years there have been an enormous number of books published. Many have been written by professional bookwriters rather than people involved with the subject. Probably the most interesting and reliable are those written by Judith Banister. There is a small bibliography at the back of this book.

CLEANING

There is more mystique and one-upmanship involved in the cleaning of silver than with any other facet of the subject. Although some polishes are better than others – by definition the word polish means to rub – the only real harm that any polish can do is to be slightly abrasive. Used sensibly, even an abrasive polish will only harm a piece by wearing away the highlights in the decoration and the marks.

Once a piece has been cleaned and polished, especially if it has been cleaned with one of the modern 'long term' polishes available on the market, it should not need another polish for a number of months. All it will need is a wash in warm water once a week; a soft drying-up cloth does the rest. For a perfect result, a cloth impregnated with silver polish can replace the drying-up cloth (these are prone to pick up small pieces of grit which can scratch fine surfaces, a problem not associated with a 'silver cloth'). The only possible achievement of a weekly polish is to rub away the finer points of the decoration which, like rubbing the marks away has a detrimental effect on the value of the piece.

There is a very simple method for cleaning the black off very dirty pieces or pieces with either cast or chased detail clogged with polish from an earlier time. The silver should be put in a basin full of hot water with dissolved washing soda. The base of the basin should be lined with aluminium foil. This method will easily remove any dirt and most of the tarnish. A soft brush, say a discarded toothbrush, can be used to remove the last traces of dirt from the decoration. After this treatment the piece will still need to be polished and the remaining tarnish removed. This is probably best done first with a polish that isn't going to clog the decoration, possibly a product like *Silver Foam*, and is used in conjunction with running warm water, followed by a rub with a silver cloth.

There are instances where problems arise over cleaning, for instance with spoons or forks used to eat or serve egg. There is a very good product available but it must be remembered that it only cleans and nothing else. The product is *Silver Dip* – often after using this liquid the piece takes on what appears to be a yellow colouration. This is due to the piece being absolutely clean, reflecting instead of its usual polish the silver's own natural yellowish colour. Once again the answer is to polish the piece with a silver cloth after washing, thus completing the work the dip has already begun.

Care of the marks should always be taken when cleaning silver. They can usually be avoided. It is worth repeating that a piece with worn marks is worth considerably less than a piece with clear marks which have been looked after. Do not stick tape over the marks as this goes rotten after a time and can stain the silver.

Silver-gilt should *never* be cleaned with anything except a soft cloth and soap and water. If, after this treatment it still does not look absolutely clean the use of a little *Silver Foam* with very hot water can often help. This is the least abrasive of all the alternatives available. Really stubborn marks can often be removed with a silk handkerchief and a little 'spit and polish'. The use of normal polishes on silver-gilt will strip the gold off in no time at all and leave the silver shining through at the points which are susceptible to wear. It is worth remembering that if a silver-gilt piece has its original gilding it will normally never be gilded anywhere that does not show or need protection from erosion (like the inside of a salt cellar) because the gilding is very costly to apply and the goldsmith anxious to conserve his gold.

Normal everyday tap-water contains a small proportion of chlorine. This is worth remembering because if silver is left to soak too long the metal will become discoloured. Short exposure is harmless.

When wrapping silver for storage it should be remembered that if some trouble is taken and the items are *well* wrapped the metal will not tarnish in store and will not need to be polished when taken out. The best method of wrapping is to use dry, acid-free paper, preferably black, which should be folded completely around the silver so as to completely isolate it from the atmosphere. This can then be given an outer wrapping of newspaper. It is *essential* that the newspaper does not come into contact with silver. The now fully-wrapped piece, insulated from the bumps by the newspaper should ideally be placed in a baize or polythene bag.

Do not wrap gold items in paper as this is bad for the metal. A soft cloth should prove an effective means of keeping gold in good condition when stored.

INSURANCE

Having taken the trouble to collect silver, spending both time and money, it would be unfortunate and unnecessary to lose it all through fire or theft. Insuring silver, especially if it is valuable is an expensive business. It is a good thing with a lot of silver to have a detailed inventory. If possible include photographs of the more valuable items. Although this may seem an extravagance it can be a very valuable investment. If properly kept up it will be useful to the police after a burglary.

Once the silver has been reliably valued and listed it is then time to get in touch with insurers. It is best to go to an insurance broker, whose job it is to get the best market terms for his customer. There is a list of brokers' addresses and telephone numbers in the 'Yellow Pages' directory. Banks can also arrange insurance cover.

The rates charged vary slightly from company to company. Any silver up to £500 in value can be insured under an ordinary householders comprehensive policy which is what most people use to cover their domestic possessions. The premium for silver within the £500 limit is very small. Over the value of £500, an 'all risks' policy is required. The silver has to be listed with the value of each individual item recorded to help both the police and insurers in the event of any fire or theft. An 'all risks' policy is only valid while the silver is in a private dwelling. The premium is just about double that under the householders comprehensive policy.

The alternative is to keep silver locked up at the bank where it can neither be used, seen, or admired and might just as well not exist apart from the satisfaction of knowing that it is there. It is normal for silver kept in the bank to be insured because the bank accepts no liability for damage by fire or loss by theft. But obviously the security of the strong room brings down the insurance premium.

OLD SHEFFIELD PLATE

A subject which tends to be surprisingly under-estimated, even today by people interested in silver, is Old Sheffield plate. In many ways, despite the lack of hallmarks, the development of Sheffield Plate from its 'discovery' through the hundred years during which it flourished helps to highlight the changing fashions and underline the redistribution of wealth that was so much a feature of the period.

Old Sheffield Plate was discovered, by mistake as we are told, by Thomas Boulsover, a cutler. At first Boulsover kept the method he had discovered of fusing silver and copper together to himself, making buttons and then other small items such as buckles and snuff boxes. The appeal of his product was immediate. When new, it was indistinguishable from real solid hallmarked silver but the cost was a mere fraction.

The invention, however, was pirated from the unfortunate Boulsover. The new leader was a gentleman by the name of Josiah Hancock. Hancock had the ambition and entrepreneurial drive that was so typical of later Sheffield and Birmingham manufacturers. Before long the products had been widened in range to include most domestic items – candlesticks, coffee pots and a host of other items.

The popularity of Sheffield Plate was immediate. Items were made that were virtually indistinguishable from their solid silver equivalents, but which could be produced for as little as a sixth of the cost. This huge disparity in prices led to a number of the plate makers marking their wares in the same manner as silver would be marked – four punches, often deliberately obscured to defraud the unwary customer.

The misuse of marks upset the wardens of the London Goldsmiths Company, who, not only could see their members losing trade to a cheaper substitute but also a new centre of machine-made silver being established which would inevitably threaten their power. The establishment of an assay office at Sheffield in 1773 put an end to the striking of marks which could be thought deliberately misleading by introducing stiff penalties for anyone found guilty of fraud.

The problems of the Sheffield Plating industry, and the methods with which they were overcome are interesting. It is obvious that demand for the product could not have been sustained had it not worn well. A piece with the underlying copper showing through was an embarassment to its once proud owner. To achieve a satisfactory life for the silver without at the same time incurring unnecessary expense by using too thick a covering of silver the formula of 7 ounces of silver for each 8 pounds of copper was evolved. Between 1760 and about 1810 the proportion of silver to copper varied greatly. Samuel Roberts (whose mark was a bell) is recorded at one time to have used 24 ounces of silver to 8 pounds of copper, but to have given this up because the improvement in the end product did not warrant the extra expense.

Another problem that for a long while gave the Sheffield Plate manufacturers problems was engraving. A plated piece just didn't have sufficient thickness of silver to withstand anything but the lightest of engraving and soon after being put into service a crest or set of initials would begin to show through the copper underneath. The answer to this was developed about the turn of the century. To ensure no problems with the engraving, a piece of solid silver would be 'let in' to a hole cut in the plated object. Often this can be noted with the naked eye as the 'let in' piece is surrounded by a fine line of solder, which tends to oxidise first when the piece gets dirty.

Other problems overcome during the first 60 years were the development of a process to plate the copper on both sides, saving the rather clumsy and very heavy back to backing that had formerly had to be used. On many pieces made in the 1780's and 90's when competition among the trade was at its highest, many small, and especially flat objects such as teapot stands and snuffer trays were made of 'one side only plate' as an additional economy measure. The problem of decoration, and its tendency to wear quickly was overcome by using silver on the borders and edges.

The death knell of Sheffield Plate was sounded in 1838 – almost exactly 100 years after its discovery. The cause was the invention of electroplating, a process by which a similar, cheaper product could be obtained. Although the new process did not really become established until the 1850's it was from 1840 that the manufacturers of Sheffield Plate found their market suddenly dwindling.

It is interesting that many of the leading producers of Sheffield Plate also made silver, often using the same machine dies for both commodities. A famous example is Matthew Boulton, whose factory and workshop produced some fine silver as well as some exceptional Sheffield Plate. Usually, makers had different marks for their silver and plated wares.

THE HALLMARKING ACT OF 1973

The more recent legislation regarding hallmarks might seem to be of small importance in comparison with the evolution of the ancient laws and customs. This might be the case but for a document known as 'Hallmarking Act of 1973', the newest addition to 600 years of up-dating and reform. Despite the date of the Act, nearly all of its provisions did not become law until 1 January 1975, and some not until 1 January 1976.

Probably the most important single element intro-duced by the new Act is that for the first time it is made mandatory for platinum to be treated in the same manner that gold and silver needs to be submitted, tried and hallmarked before being put on sale. That platinum had not been included as an assayable metal some time ago is in many ways surprising. For the last 60 years the metal has been of increasing importance to the jewellery trade as well as being a noble metal like gold which resists the attack of all acids and is unaffected by air.

The history of platinum, its discovery and more recently its great use is somewhat obscure. It is probable that the Spaniards during their conquest of Central and Southern America in the sixteenth century were the first Europeans to encounter platinum. There are references to a metal which they found which could not be melted in the goldsmiths' furnaces – platinum has a very high melting point – $1755°$ Centigrade as opposed to $1064°$ for gold and 961 for silver. The next important mention of the metal is in 1750 when a Doctor Brownrigg, who had been sent some by his relative, Charles Wood, a metallurgist, gave a piece to the Royal Society naming it platina del Pinto (little silver from the river Pinto).

Platinum was used by Russia as a substitute for silver in coinage from 1828 through to 1845. The platinum was mined in the Ural Mountains which remained the main source of the metal until the discovery of deposits in Canada in the late 1920s. It is also found in the Transvaal in South Africa. It is surprising that one of the principal sources of platinum is from the residue left after extracting nickle from its ores, though there is only one part of platinum to two million parts of nickle!

The reason for platinum's expanding use in jewellery is that when alloyed with iridium (the new legislation limits the alloy to 5 per cent) it has most of the properties of gold but is much more resistant to wear. It is for this reason that one of the more common uses is for standards for weights and measures.

The 1973 Hallmarking Act specifies that it is illegal to describe any item as silver, gold or platinum which is *unhallmarked* in the course of business or trade. This sounds simple but by 'unhallmarked', the Act means that the item being described does not bear the 'approved' hallmarks under the Act. Accompanying the approved marks must be the sponsor's mark; the *new* term for what is commonly known as a maker's mark. This was introduced as a reflection on the modern methods of large-scale factory manufacture.

For a hallmark to be regarded as approved it has to conform to a very simple set of rules. The hallmark has to have been struck by an official assay office under the legislation which was in force at the time of striking. This includes marks struck by the Dublin assay office before 1923. There is at this point a very interesting qualification, introduced it appears as the result of the Treaty of Rome. This is the incorporation under the term 'approved', of a provision at a future date for 'approved' to be taken to cover marks struck abroad under an international convention. Is it possible that in the distant future there might be a European hallmarking system?

The description, 'unhallmarked', under the Act extends in certain circumstances to cover pieces which either are, or were properly hallmarked originally, but which have had their hallmarks changed, defaced or added to without the written permission of an assay office; or where the nature of the piece has been changed. There is an exception made in the case of metal which is in the course of breaking – scrap metal suitable only for melting and remanufacture. Should the alteration increase the weight of the piece concerned, then, regardless of whether the use of the piece remains the same or not, if the increase in weight is 50 per cent or more the piece is considered by the Act to be unhallmarked. It is quite in order for an assay office when giving its written permission for a piece to be altered to stipulate that once altered the piece should be resubmitted for assay in the same way as a new piece.

The 1973 Hallmarking Act spends some time on the subject of the quality and type of solder which may be used in the manufacture of a piece. It stipulates that no article may be struck with the approved hallmarks unless the assay office is convinced that the amount of solder used is not excessive; and that no solder of a lower standard of purity than the piece is used for strengthening, weighting or filling a piece. The Act however allows the use of solder for small joining tasks which is of a slightly lower standard of purity and therefore with a slightly lower melting point than the main object. The only exception is platinum. This can be soldered with any combination of palladium, silver or gold still – but it has to be 95 per cent pure.

Another modernising feature of the Act is the way in which it quietly replaces the *carat* method of grading gold with a decimal method which simply mentions the parts of pure gold in a thousand – hence 12 carat (half the 'pure' 24 carats) would become .500. The standards that are recognised by the new legislation are listed below with their old carat designation, their equivalent standard of purity and the marks used from 1 January 1975 on both British and imported wares:

Carat	Standard	Made in UK (+ town mark)	Imported
9	375	A Crown and figures 375	figures 375
14	585	A Crown and figures 585	figures 585
18	750	A Crown and figures 750	figures 750
22	916.6	A Crown and figures 916	figures 916

It is pleasing to note that the 22 carat designation defeated the neat decimal figures twice. It is not often that the decimal 0.6 is found rounded down rather than up. There is yet more in the way of inconsistency. In the list of permissible solder, although the solder for 22 ct (916.6 gold) is permitted to be 750 (18 ct) and that for filigree or watchcases in 750 it is 740, for white gold of 750 the solder must be of a minimum 500, the discarded 12 ct! The amount of the impurities allowed in the solder for sterling (925) silver is a full 35 per cent (350), a useful differential.

One part of the new Act that is very relevant is the provisions for anybody caught trying to contravene it. There are stringent penalties now for the person convicted of a hallmarking counterfeiting offence, making a false die or mark, removing a mark from a previously assayed piece, affixing a mark taken from a previously assayed piece to anything, selling or giving away a false die or punch or even 'without lawful authority or excuse' possessing a piece with a fake mark or just the punch! The penalties for these crimes are amazingly high. The maximum penalty on summary conviction is £400, while for conviction on indictment the guilty offender can be gaoled for up to ten years. It is worth noting that included in the above crimes is the offence of faking the maker's (or sponsor's) mark.

In this event, however, the Act softens the blow by including a series of paragraphs to protect the individual both from his ignorance and from the cunning forger of past times. Undoubtedly the most important protection for the private individual is the paragraph which states:

'. . . An assay office shall not, otherwise than by leave of the owner or other person appearing to have control of any article, obliterate any ancient mark but shall cancel the same in a manner as authorised . . .'

The term, 'Ancient Mark' has a meaning of far reaching consequence. It is defined in the Act as a mark having the character of a hallmark appearing to an assay office to have been struck or incorporated (in the case of transposed marks) before 22 December 1854, regardless of whether the piece as such was within the law at the time that it was made or marked. The only exception is in the case of pieces which have since been the subject of alteration.

The far reaching effect of this statement mean that for the first time such irregularities as the 'duty dodgers' of the 1720's and 30's and the quantities of silver with pseudo-hallmarks that were produced in the colonies during the last quarter of the eighteenth century and the first half of the nineteenth can be freely sold and described in Britain without breaking any law. The new law does not, however, cover the majority of pieces,

149

which can properly be described as fakes and which were made during the last quarter of the nineteenth century, simply to deceive.

Other new requirements include provision that any dealer, even if dealing exclusively with the trade has to keep on exhibition at all times, in a conspicuous position in a part of his premises to which his customers are commonly admitted, a notice or sign in a form supplied by the new Hallmarking Council (who may make a reasonable charge for the notice) describing all the approved hallmarks and with such explanation of the marks as the council think fit. It is made an offence for a dealer to fail to keep the notice on exhibition. The common sense behind this requirement is obvious. Not only will the notice be a useful on-the-spot reference for the customer but it also acts a form of long-term easy education for the buying public.

The British Hallmarking Council, as set up under the Act came into being on 1 January 1974, thus giving itself a year's start on the other major provisions of the Act. The council consists of between 16 and 19 members, 6 appointed by the assay offices (two each for London and Birmingham, one for Edinburgh and Sheffield) and 10 by the Secretary of State. Of the members appointed by the Secretary of State a maximum of four are allowed to be involved in trading or manufacture of precious metals while three have to be people involved in activities concerned with consumer protection.

The constitution of the council provides for it to co-opt a maximum of two extra members. The only assay office employee eligible to sit on the council is the clerk to the assay office. Should one of the six assay office appointed members be elected chairman to the council, then there is provision for a replacement member (16 plus two co-opted members plus an assay office appointee as chairman makes the maximum 19 members). Any assay office is entitled to send a representative to speak at a meeting of the council. The last point concerning the constitution is that the council is financed by the assay offices.

The powers of the council are very basic: to fix the charges levied on pieces brought into assay offices for assay; advise the Secretary of State on any conclusions the council might come to relating to the amendment of the law; advise on the amalgamation or closure of the existing assay offices or the establishment of new ones as the need may occur; institute proceedings against people considered to have offended against the Act; direct the manner, equipment and procedures that are to be used either by all the assay offices or by a specific assay office. To all these powers the assay offices have the right of appeal to the Secretary of State. The council and Secretary of State also have the power at any time to apply the provisions of this Act to any other metal than platinum, gold or silver.

The council is bound by the Act to prepare an annual report of its performance, including a record of all the questions with which the council has been concerned and appear to it to be of general interest. It is the duty of the council, on application, to furnish any individual with a copy of this report on request. But, the council has the right to charge for the service.

It is not until the seven schedules attached to the Act are examined that one of the more surprising changes is discovered. Under the list of approved hallmarks the first three towns are as expected: London – a leopard's head, Birmingham – an anchor and Edinburgh – a castle. But when it comes to Sheffield the approved mark

151

listed is a rose, presumably a York rose. The reason for this sad break with tradition was almost certainly the use in the past of a crown as both the Sheffield town mark and the mark accompanying the gold standard mark.

The duties of assay offices are also listed among the schedules to the Act. For example when on receipt of any article submitted for assay and hallmarking an assay office suspects that anything other than precious metal of the prescribed standard it can order the piece to be cut (e.g. if they suspect the handle of a beer-mug to have been filled with lead) and if when the piece has been cut they find '. . . any such other material . . .' the article has to be broken and defaced, it, or the value of it being forfeit to the assay office. Should the assay office cut a piece that is innocent of such trickery it is then liable to pay damages to the owner. If in the normal course of assay a piece is found to be of less than the minimum standard permitted it has to be returned unmarked to its owner after payment of the assay fee. In the case of a new ware the assay office has the power not only to break the one offending piece but also any others submitted in the same parcel.

The assay office also has the right to '. . . cause to be drawn, scraped, cut or otherwise removed from the article such quantity of precious metal or take such other sample or do such other thing as may be necessary to enable an accurate assay to be made . . .'. The samples taken for assay become the property of the assay office, being kept towards the general expenses of the office. It is usual on flat bottomed antique pieces of silver to be able clearly to identify the 'scrape' where silver has been taken for assay. With modern methods this is only very rarely possible.

Although much of the tradition has been removed in

the new legislation it is interesting that the Royal Mint (Her Majesty's Mint) still has the right to visit any assay office to inspect, ascertain and assess the accuracy and efficiency of the methods and procedures used in the assay. Should the Royal Mint not approve of any of the procedures it then has to notify both the assay office and the council as to its suggestions and recommendations. For this service Her Majesty's Mint is entitled to make a charge to the assay office in question. Finally, once every 14 months the Queen's Assay Master is required to draw up a report on the assay department of each office, and having sent copies first to the assay offices and the council, send a copy to the deputy master at the Mint. This procedure dates back to the origins of hallmarking.

The number of previous Acts of Parliament relating to hallmarking that are repealed by the new legislation is a staggering 22, with a further 12 Acts being modified in some way. Among the casualties are some historic pieces of legislation:

Act for encouraging the bringing in of wrought plate to be coined	1696
Plate Duty Act	1719
Plate Offences Act	1738
The Silver Plate Act	1790
The Plate Assay (Ireland) Act	1807
The Plate (Scotland) Act	1836
The Plate (Sheffield and Birmingham) Act	1772
The Glasgow Assay Office Act	1819

There are other changes to the traditional hallmarks which, like the Sheffield crown turning into a rose, are not mentioned specifically but simply listed in a schedule.

One of the more logical changes is the dropping of the lion's head erased Britannia accompanying mark. This is simply replaced by the town mark (its original 1696 function). The dropping of the thistle mark in Edinburgh is also reasonable. The lion rampant is not only universally recognised as representing Scotland, but is one of the marks of the now closed Glasgow assay office. In Birmingham, the town mark is struck on the side in the case of gold and platinum, and on the vertical for silver – a situation not considered necessary elsewhere.

CHRONOLOGICAL TABLES

CHRONOLOGICAL TABLE (1)

ENGLAND
(925.00 standard)

LONDON		PROVINCES
1180	Goldsmiths fined for not holding King's licence.	
1238	Six Wardens appointed to oversee craft.	
1327	Goldsmiths receive Royal Charter.	
1423	Leopard's Head mark introduced, makers' mark made legal necessity.	'Divers Touches' granted to Bristol, Coventry, Lincoln, Newcastle upon Tyne, Norwich, Salisbury and York.
1462	Goldsmiths become corporate body.	
1478	Variable date-letter introduced.	
1536	Dissolution of the Monasteries.	Dissolution of the Monasteries.
1544	Lion Passant introduced.	
LONDON		PROVINCES
1642	Civil War.	Civil War.
1660	Restoration.	Restoration.
1696	Britannia Standard introduced. Re-coinage commenced.	Britannia Standard introduced. Re-coinage commenced.
1700		Provision for Assay Offices at Bristol, Chester, Exeter, Norwich and York.
1702		Provision for Assay Office at Newcastle upon Tyne
1717		Assay Office at York closed.

155

	LONDON	PROVINCES
1720	Sterling Standard re-introduced. Duty of 6d an ounce started.	Sterling Standard brought back. Duty of 6d an ounce introduced.
1758	Duty taken off.	Duty taken off.
1773		Assay Offices opened at Birmingham and Sheffield.
1776	LONDON	PROVINCES Assay Office at York re-opened.
1784	King's Head duty mark introduced with return of the 6d duty.	King's Head Duty mark introduced with return of 6d duty.
1856		Office at York closed.
1882		Office at Exeter closed.
1884		Office at Newcastle upon Tyne closed.
1890	Duty taken off; duty mark discontinued.	Duty taken off, duty mark discontinued.
1962		Office at Chester closed.

CHRONOLOGICAL TABLE (2)

SCOTLAND
(916.6 standard)

EDINBURGH		PROVINCES
1457	Deacon appointed to place his mark alongside maker's mark on a tested piece.	
1555	Standard 'Restored' to 916.6.	Standard 'Restored' to 916.6.
1586	Goldsmiths granted their first Letters Patent.	
1681	Variable date letter introduced.	

1707	Act of Union.	Act of Union.
1720	Duty of 6d an ounce introduced.	
1758	Duty removed.	
1784	King's Head duty mark introduced with the re-imposition of 6d duty.	

EDINBURGH		PROVINCES
1819		Assay Office at Glasgow (925 standard).
1836	925 Standard made universal in United Kingdom.	
1890	Duty revoked and duty mark discontinued.	

CHRONOLOGICAL TABLE (3)

IRELAND
(925.00 standard)

DUBLIN		PROVINCES
1605	Maker's mark made legal obligation.	
1606	Mark of Lion, Harp and Castle introduced for assayed plate.	
1637	Goldsmiths granted charter of incorporation. Mark of Crowned Harp introduced for assayed plate.	
1638	Variable date-letters introduced.	
1730	Duty of 6d an ounce introduced, also figure of Hibernia duty mark.	
1752	Made illegal to sell plate without Hibernia mark.	

1784		Assay Office opened at New Geneva. Assay Office at New Geneva closed.
DUBLIN		PROVINCES
1801	Act of Union.	Act of Union.
1807	English duty introduced with King's Head duty mark.	
1890	Duty revoked: duty mark discontinued.	
1923	All plate after this date foreign in respect of Customs and Excise of the United Kingdom.	

BIBLIOGRAPHY

General:
Report of the Departmental Committee on Hallmarking, H.M.S.O. 1959 (137 pp)
Silver, Gerald Taylor, Pelican, 1956 (302 pp)
English Silver, Judith Bannister, Ward Lock, 1965 (256 pp)
English Domestic Silver, Charles Oman, A & C Black, 1934 (240 pp)
Three Centuries of English Domestic Silver, Bernard and Therle Hughes, Lutterworth, 1952 (248 pp)
English Goldsmiths and their Marks, Sir Charles Jackson, Macmillan, 1921 (747 pp)
1973 Hallmarking Act.

Special Periods:
Adam Silver, Robert Rowe, Faber, 1965 (190 pp)
Huguenot Silver in England 1688–1727, J. Hayward, Faber, 1959 (185 pp)
Also Victoria and Albert Museum series of Picture Books

Special Subjects:
Silver Boxes, Eric Delieb, Herbert Jenkins, 1968 (120 pp)
English Vinaigrettes, E. Ellenbogen, Cambridge, 1956 (39 pp)
Bottle Tickets, Victoria and Albert Museum, 1958 (31 pp)

Price Guides:
Price Guide to Antique Silver, Ian Harris, Baron, 1968 (510 pp)

INDEX

159